FRUIT OF THE SPIRIT:
AN ORTHODOX ANTHOLOGY

ORTHODOX LOGOS PUBLISHING

FRUIT OF THE SPIRIT:
AN ORTHODOX ANTHOLOGY

by Deacon David Lochbihler, J.D.

Front Cover photograph by Oxana Ware
Back Cover photograph by Reverend Christopher Bear
About the Author photograph by Micah Marie Friedrich

Book cover design and interior layout by Max Mendor

Publishers Maxim Hodak & Max Mendor

© 2023, Deacon David Lochbihler, J.D.

© 2023, Orthodox Logos Publishing,

The Netherlands

www.orthodoxlogos.com

ISBN: 978-1-80484-104-4
ISBN: 978-1-80484-105-1

This book is in copyright. No part of this publication may be reproduced, stored in a retrieval system or transmitted in any form or by any means without the prior permission in writing of the publisher, nor be otherwise circulated in any form of binding or cover other than that in which it is published without a similar condition, including this condition, being imposed on the subsequent purchaser.

CONTENTS

ACKNOWLEDGEMENTS 11

ABOUT THIS BOOK 16

PROLOGUE
OUR FIRST CHRISTMAS TOGETHER 17

   CHAPTER ONE
   LOVE 21

   CHAPTER TWO
   JOY 34

   CHAPTER THREE
   PEACE 39

   CHAPTER FOUR
   LONGSUFFERING 45

   CHAPTER FIVE
   KINDNESS 54

   CHAPTER SIX
   GOODNESS 62

   CHAPTER SEVEN
   FAITHFULNESS 68

   CHAPTER EIGHT
   GENTLENESS 83

   CHAPTER NINE
   SELF-CONTROL 91

   COMMENCEMENT IN CHRIST 102

EPILOGUE
THE JOY OF ORTHODOXY 113

ABOUT THE AUTHOR 120

DEACON DAVID LOCHBIHLER, J.D.

FRUIT OF THE SPIRIT:
AN ORTHODOX ANTHOLOGY

ORTHODOX LOGOS PUBLISHING

To
Jacquelyn Amanda for inspiring me to Write,
Langley Georgia for encouraging me to Write,
and
Lucia Marie and Maximus Ashby for Writing

Fruits of the Spirit
by
Millie Ruth Frazier

Love, Joy, Peace, Longsuffering, Kindness,
Goodness, Faithfulness, Gentleness, and Self-control.
These are the Fruits of the Spirit.

Love obeys God.
Joy watches new puppies being born.
Peace hears the ocean waves.
Longsuffering endures.
Kindness cares for others.
Goodness has a good attitude.
Faithfulness has a good relationship with God.
Gentleness speaks kindly to those around you.
Self-control controls your temper.

Love, Joy, Peace, Longsuffering, Kindness,
Goodness, Faithfulness, Gentleness, and Self-control.
For these are the Fruits of the Spirit!

ACKNOWLEDGEMENTS

A special thank you and warm welcome to His Eminence Metropolitan Saba Esper, Archbishop of New York and Metropolitan of All North America, as he visited Saint Patrick Orthodox Church in Virginia for Sung Vespers and a potluck dinner on Monday 22 May 2023. Our beloved Metropolitan joyfully reminded us, "The purpose of the Christian life is to acquire the Holy Spirit in us, to be children of God." Thank you also to His Grace Bishop John Abdalah for ordaining me at Saint Patrick Orthodox Church while celebrating the Feast of Saint Patrick on Sunday 17 March 2019. Bishop John recently visited our church during Pentecost and shared these wise words with our precious people in the pews: "God knows that the world is complicated and complex; but He is with us and will guide us, if we allow ourselves to get out of our own way and allow Him to love us and show Himself through us."

Our kind bishop also blessed us with these most memorable words: "This community is a miraculous one." Truly blessed at age sixty-six to find myself serving at both the best church and the finest school in the world.

David and Jo Thoburn hired me to teach fourth grade at The Fairfax Christian School in Dulles, Virginia, eight years ago. I am eternally grateful to them and my esteemed colleague, David McElfresh, for his positive recommendation leading to my hiring and for welcoming my students into his high school Chemistry laboratory to teach them how to compete successfully in the Science Fair each spring. My life was changed forever upon landing this most magnificent assignment teaching fourth-grade scholars at the very best school in the Commonwealth of Virginia.

An author must never forget his friends from university shaping his life forever. Thank you to the Sorin Seven from the University of Notre Dame: Doctor Dick Duffey, Doctor Mark Heberlein, Steve Jehl, Father Bob Loughery, Paul Peralta, Rick Remick, and Kevin Ryan of blessed memory. My freshman roommate Tom Rigsby and two Fighting Irish friends continuing their commitment to academic excellence with me in graduate studies at the University of Texas, Diego Peña and Bob Savage, remain lifelong friends. Special thanks also to CBS political analyst Robert Costa and architect and author Michael Molinelli for their enthusiastic encouragement. Graduating from Notre Dame with Hall-of-Fame quarterback Joe Montana, perhaps the greatest player in N.F.L history, and driving cross-country to witness the memorable Cotton Bowl battles of 1978 and 1979, a National Championship victory and perhaps the greatest comeback in college football history, respectively, brought an abundance of joy into my heart to last a lifetime.

As a varsity high school coach nearly two decades ago, my teams at Bethlehem Baptist Christian Academy and Fair Oaks Academy in Fairfax, Virginia, inspired me by capturing four Northern Virginia Independent Athletic Conference championships in five years. Soccer's fabulous Four Horsemen – Jae, Will, Danny, and Matt – stole the crown against an undefeated and highly-skilled perennial championship rival after double overtime by delivering a perfect penalty kick shootout, and on the basketball court, my Assistant Coach James G. Slater and I celebrated three magnificent playdown and conference championship runs. Danny da Prodigy, Matt, Jae, Andrew, and Josh won the first with a dramatic dive and a flurry of threes; Cristos, David the Pistol, Sam, James, and Darryl captured the second with a 49-47 buzzer beater; and Cristos, Bobak, Daniel, Tyler, and James staged a dramatic 48-43 come-from-behind victory to steal the third. Thank you to all my players and assistant coaches during the past three decades, far too many winners and Christ Champions to mention by name.

Innumerable pen pals bring immeasurable joy to my heart. My most famous pen pal was Metropolitan Kallistos Ware of blessed memory, kind enough to send a few thoughtful postcards from Oxford, England, during the early years of my entry into Orthodoxy a decade ago. Franciscan priests Father Walter Dolan of blessed memory, Father Zachary Hayes of blessed memory, Father Henry Willenborg, Father Mike Haney, Father Chuck Faso, Father Don Blaeser, and Father Tom Nairn of the Sacred Heart Province corresponded faithfully for more than three decades. Lindsay Marie and I have been premier pen pals for nearly a quarter of a century. Besides sending pen pal letters and postcards, Craft Captain Luci Marie planned countless Sunday School team-taught classes. Maggie McLaurin continues penning long letters after many years, and I still receive loads of letters from my prayerful pen pals Maximus Ashby, a sports superstar, and Millie Ruth, a prestigious poet.

I am eternally grateful to Coptic priest Father Anthony Messeh, Father Alexander Atty of blessed memory, Father Peter Gillquist of blessed memory, and Father Patrick Cardine, for being my first four contacts guiding and inspiring me into Orthodoxy.

My wonder-full family gathered last month to celebrate Mom's one-hundred-and-first birthday, and there is much joy whenever I visit my older siblings Fred, Lyn, and Vince and their families. Each day I also pray by name for Whitney and Judy, Angela Marie and Kevin, Grant and Nolan, Stephanie Lynn and Isaac, Brett Jordan, Fred and Tania, and Frederick Fuechee and Leilala Hli Nra.

Finally, a profound personal and professional thank you to Subdeacon Scott Richardson, my faithful American advisor and editor recently returning home after completing his fourth Camino de Santiago pilgrimage in Spain. Holy and heartfelt love and appreciation to Maxim Hodak and Max Mendor of Stichting Orthodox Logos and Ksenia Papazova, the Managing Editor of Glagoslav Publications, in Nederland, for your admirable assistance in publishing my five theological books. Your deep commitment to our beloved Orthodox faith inspires.

Life is a most miraculous mystery. Baptized at Saint Patrick Catholic Church in Indiana as an infant in 1957, I was chrismated at Saint Patrick Orthodox Church in Virginia in 2013. "May the God of hope fill you with joy and peace in your faith, that by the power of the Holy Spirit, your whole life and outlook may be radiant with hope" (Romans 15:13 PHILLIPS). We all are too, too blessed.

Friends in Jesus and Mary, Angels and Saints,
Deacon David Lochbihler
Saint Patrick Orthodox Church
Friday 8 September 2023
Feast of the Nativity of the Blessed Virgin Mary
Consecrated with Chrism Oil a Decade Earlier
orthodoxdeacondavid@gmail.com

ABOUT THIS BOOK

All of our lives strive to mirror the Fruit of the Spirit described in Galatians 5:22-23. Prior to becoming a published author, I submitted articles to *The Word*, the premier periodical of the Antiochian Orthodox Christian Archdiocese of North America, and the magazine published five of my essays. As an anthology of Orthodox essays, this work utilizes a format distinct from my other four books. As separate articles spanning several years, the chapters of this book stand independently and sometimes overlap. For example, some chapters use footnotes, while others place citations within parentheses inside the text. As distinct articles, the chapters in this book need not be read in succession. I hope and pray various chapters within this book truly touch your heart and draw you closer to union and communion with our Uncreated God.

PROLOGUE

OUR FIRST CHRISTMAS TOGETHER

(*The Word* published "Our First Christmas Together"
in May 2015.)

"The authors of the Holy Writ boldly proclaim this most scandalous message that the uncreated eternal Holy God would become, could become flesh and remain flesh for all eternity. And in so doing would sanctify and make divine that which is created." Father Patrick preached this message at the Midnight Divine Liturgy during our first Christmas together in our new church sanctuary at Saint Patrick Orthodox Church in Bealeton, Virginia.

Our new church lent itself to the mystery of the Incarnation during our first Christmas together. Two images come to mind. First and most obvious, and rather humorous, was that of the fattest Christmas tree you have ever seen, reaching up to the ceiling and covering almost a third of the floor space to the left of the altar. In their written reflections about the feast, two of our youth thought like me and readily remembered our "very fat tree."

The second, more profound image I recall was the many lit candles. Standing serenely in our new sanctuary on

Christmas Eve, I immediately noticed the beautiful light of the many candles proclaiming the First Coming of the Light of the World. What would life be like without this Divine Light? Father Patrick preached at our first Midnight Mass, "He was born in a cave because we were trapped in a darkness, born among beasts because we had become irrational beasts, bound by cloths because we have been bound by sin, laid in a feed trough because His flesh is true food and His blood true drink for the life of the world."

Our new church building was so beautiful during our first Midnight Mass together. I asked our people what stood out for them during this historic first for our congregation. Mark, an attorney, jumped right to the heart of the matter: "The Eucharist." Born in the darkness of midnight, we now live in the light of day, because "he who eats My flesh and drinks My blood abides in Me, and I in him" (John 6:56, NASB). The "simplicity" of our first Christmas together stood out for Lisa, a nurse. As Saint Paul struggled to keep the church in Corinth focused on orthodoxy, he spoke about darkness and sin and challenged them to choose light and holiness: "But I am afraid that, as the serpent deceived Eve by his craftiness, your minds will be led astray from the simplicity and purity of devotion to Christ" (2 Corinthians 11:3, NASB). Leila, creative and artistic, rejoiced at the beauty of the "sound" within our new sanctuary. Moving from the back of a rented antique store to the ceilings of a new sanctuary truly enhanced our worship experience, the "amazing acoustics" giving the singing of Khouria Kerrie and the choir, in Leila's words, "a richer, deeper sound." As King David called the people of Israel, so, too, we are encouraged, to "sing unto the LORD, O ye saints of His, and give thanks at the remembrance of His holiness" (Psalm 30:4, KJV).

Our youth loved and cherished our first Christmas together as much as their parents. The beautifully rich acoustics touched the heart of Abigail: "The songs we sung, I really thought about it, and I think I really came closer to God." Elizabeth "felt the Holy Spirit come into me and fill me with the Christmas spirit." She also loved Luke's Gospel read by Deacon Douglas: "Just hearing the birth of Jesus made me smile." Granted our years worshipping at the back of the antique store still were special, but Siena for the first time could joyfully declare, "This Christmas I got to celebrate in a *church*."

Mary, one of our youth leaders, summarized the myriad feelings within the hearts of both young and old in this our first Christmas together at Saint Patrick Orthodox Church: "Christmas is always such a humbling and serene service. However, as we celebrated the Nativity Feast for the first time in our new building, in our own building, it seemed to rise to an even higher level of spirituality. There was a calm about the nave. The choir sounded especially angelic as their sound echoed through the church. There was a feeling of peace, a sense of belonging that seemed to hang over the building. We know the church is represented by the people and not necessarily the building, but the beauty and serenity of Christmas Mass proved the glory and joy that comes with a holy house of worship."

"And the Word became flesh and dwelt among us, and we beheld His glory, the glory as of the only begotten of the

Father, full of grace and truth (John 1:14, NKJV). Father Patrick's sermon brought us back to the significance of the essential mystery of our Orthodox faith, the Incarnation: "God has become a part of this creation without ceasing to be God and all the world has been changed and made holy. The seas have been delivered of the serpent; blood and breath, and sky and earth have been made new because God has become flesh and has sanctified all flesh. His descent into the watery womb of the Holy Virgin and His descent into the watery tomb of the River Jordan have redeemed the waters themselves. The created and the uncreated have been united in the Virgin's womb and nothing remains the same, all has become sacred, this is what happened when God became man."

Father Patrick's beautiful daughter Olivia Jane was sick at home and missed our first Christmas together. Steeped in the truth of Orthodoxy, she felt deeply saddened knowing what she was missing but celebrated and rejoiced with us nonetheless: "I imagine everything coming together to make a beautiful and memorable first Christmas at St. Patrick Orthodox Church. And most importantly, it showed what Advent, Christmas, and Epiphany are all about: GOD."

CHAPTER ONE

LOVE

As a fourth-grade teacher at a magnificent Christian school in Northern Virginia, I love the month of June, the launch of The Great Summer Vacation. Summer for educators is a relaxing time of travel to both deepen our love for family and nurture lifelong friendships. Father's Day also lands in June, and Father's Day celebrations after our Orthodox Divine Liturgies across the world renew wonderful joyful childhood memories while, for so many of us remembering death, rekindling sad yet hopeful recollections of our beloved fathers falling asleep in Christ.

Dad lay on his deathbed. The year was 1983.

Having the best Dad in the world makes for the most wonder-full childhood memories. Dad came home after work one day with the gift of our very first baseball cards. My first card was a 1966 Topps Willie Mays! Dad also brought home a simple dollar baseball card game, and we played season after season with our baseball cards, keeping stats and enjoying countless hours of family fun.

Our family baseball card games became more advanced as we children grew older. In one strategic game, you selected your own players, and Dad looked back to his own childhood half-a-century earlier and played our games with his favourite team, the 1919 Chicago White Sox. Dad grew up in Chicago and went with the South Siders. For those of you unfamiliar with baseball history, some of my Dad's favourite players cavorted with gamblers, threw the World Series, and were kicked out of major league baseball for life. As we played our baseball board games, these disgraced baseball players fondly recalled from Dad's early childhood were the stars of his team.

Dad took my brother Vince and me to our first major league baseball game on Saturday 22 April 1966 at Wrigley Field in Chicago. When you are nine years old and you first see the beautiful green field and majestic ivy outfield fence of a stadium, after a few years of watching games on a black-and-white television, you experience a timeless memory to last a lifetime. My brother Vince and I brought our gloves to the ballpark, and as we walked to our seats, we looked around in awe, as if entering for the first time the most magnificent Gothic cathedral. Arriving late, we walked slowly to our seats, still staring in wonder at the colorful excitement of our first major league baseball game. All of a sudden, unbeknownst to us, a foul ball flew our way. As we stood in wonder and stared into space, mitts in hand, we were unaware of the growing fervor surrounding us. I recall Dad's hand reaching near the ground to pick up the baseball a split second too late. Baseball mitts aren't much help if you fail to keep your eye on the ball! For two consecutive ballgames, we sat on the edge of our seats waiting for another foul ball, a wait that would last more than fifteen years.

Dad drove Vince and me one day after school to meet a young major league baseball player from the Cincinnati Reds named Pete Rose. During our car ride from Elwood Drive to *Main Auto Sports Shop* in downtown Fort Wayne, Vince and I excitedly shared dozens of questions we would ask Mr. Rose with Dad. When we finally shook hands with the first major leaguer we met personally, we stood still in silence, completely speechless and overcome by the moment. Dad tried to help us by asking, "Boys, do you have any questions for Mr. Rose?" All we could do is shake our heads in stunned silence.

Mom and Dad took us to Concordia Senior College to hear Senator Robert F. Kennedy, an aspiring presidential candidate during the tumultuous 1968 campaign. The year 1968 changed American history and touched our lives forever, breaking through the suburban safety of Fort Wayne. During my fifth-grade year, the United States found herself in political upheaval. Mom and Dad did their best to keep us safe and protect us from the turmoil of those troubling times. On Wednesday 23 April 1968, just a few weeks after the assassination of Dr. Martin Luther King, Jr. in Memphis, and a little more than a month before his own untimely death in Los Angeles, Senator Kennedy visited my hometown, and Dad got a press copy of the speech as a keepsake. Our entire family was lucky enough to sit at the right place at the right time to be able to snap a few close-up photographs and shake the Senator's hand.

Beginning in about my fourth-grade year, Dad, now nearly sixty years old, and I began hanging out together every Saturday. We started our weekend adventure at Dad's office. While Dad worked on any newly-sold insurance policies, I calculated batting averages for the hitters and earned run averages (with the help of a slide rule) for the pitchers. After a brief stop at *Arnold Palmer Dry Cleaners*, we headed for the Fort Wayne Public Library, and while Dad picked up some books, I headed for the sports section, Dewey Decimal Section 796, to read about my favourite baseball, football, and basketball stars. We then would drive to Northcrest Shopping Center and later, better yet, to an amazing new thing in America, the indoor mall, at Glenbrook. We concluded our fine morning routine together with a visit to Ponderosa Steakhouse. Dad ordered the Number One Sirloin Strip, and I ordered the Number Two Rib Eye. Our simple yet very special Saturday adventures continued for about seven years until my junior year in high school, ordinary weekends offering precious lifelong memories.

Although our whole family enjoyed traveling together to McCormick's Creek State Park in Indiana during our summer vacations, I alone inherited from Dad his love for Chicago's struggling sports teams. Like Dad, I became what famous baseball owner and entrepreneur Bill Veeck called "a long-suffering White Sox fan." We also loved the Chicago Bears football team and travelled to Rensselaer, Indiana, to watch the Bears' summer training camp at Saint Joseph's College. Dad took a memorable photograph of me with the legendary linebacker Dick Butkus, and in my small, orange Chicago Bears Press Guide from 1968, with Dad's help, I got autographs from many players including running backs Gale Sayers and Brian Piccolo, their friendship featured a few years later in a fantastic family film, *Brian's Song*.

Dad gave the best birthday present ever to me. When I was thirteen years old, Dad and I drove to Indianapolis during my birthday weekend to watch my favourite player, Rick Mount of the Indiana Pacers basketball team, play a couple games. Dad knew Rick Mount was my hero, and during one of our drives to see the Bears, we made a quick stop to Purdue University just to take a quick look inside the arena where Rick played college ball. It was exciting to see the professional players battle in Indianapolis, and seeing my boyhood hero on the basketball court made this birthday most memorable.

After a few years, I followed my brother Fred's footprints and enrolled at the University of Notre Dame, and Mom and Dad retired to Sun City Center, Florida. During one summer vacation, I remember playing Dad with one of our most skillful baseball board games. This particular game required a lot of thought and strategy. As a college student, I played this game from childhood with much ease. The game seemed so simple to me, and I crushed "the old man" by double digits, showing no mercy. Many years later, reflecting upon my life and the many good times and long hours spent with Dad, I thought back to our many baseball card and board game seasons together, and something finally occurred to me. Looking back, it seems like Dad won most all of our regular baseball seasons before the playdowns, but somehow, when it came time for the World Series, I always seemed to capture the championship. It dawned on me Dad most likely let me win and become champion at the end of every one of our seasons. I then recalled how I mercilessly ran up the score against Dad when I was in college, and I felt quite ashamed.

After Notre Dame, I attended the University of Texas School of Law, and Dad was there for my graduation in Austin. His visit was memorable. We watched the Texas Longhorns play a college baseball game, and I sat between Dad and my friend Stacey. A towering foul ball touched the sky and was heading straight towards us. Here was another chance to catch a foul ball, this time without a mitt. Leaning towards Stacey, I reached both hands just above her head. The ball hit my right hand and careened about ten feet in the air, a clear error on a dropped foul ball as the crowd collectively sighed. As I rubbed my hand to get rid of the sting, Stacey asked, "Did you hurt your hand?"

Dad quipped, "The only thing he hurt was his pride."

During that Texas visit, Dad asked me to drive to a neighborhood, and I parked the car as Dad went into one of the suburban homes. Dad spent about a half-hour with an old baseball player named Bibb Falk. Mr. Falk, now in his eighties, was Dad's favourite player when he was a kid. One year after the 1919 Black Sox scandal, Mr. Falk joined the White Sox as a rookie, when Dad was eight. Dad came out of the house with an old autographed photograph of his boyhood hero.

Cancer struck Dad soon after his trip to Texas. Cancer is a most hated and dreadful disease. Any family suffering through this scourge understands the deep pain. As Dad's condition continued to deteriorate, Mom sought a pathway towards hope. Mom saw a segment on the television news show called *20/20* featuring a Roman Catholic priest, Father Dennis Kelleher of blessed memory, engaged in a national faith healing ministry. A healing Mass was scheduled in

Chicago, and Mom and Dad flew into O'Hare Airport with our family gathering from across the country to attend.

I cannot recall ever seeing Dad sick a day in his life, and it was quite jarring to see him quite tired and sickly arriving at O'Hare in a wheelchair. Our family drove to the church. During the healing service, anyone wanting a blessing lined up in front of the altar rail, and Father Kelleher laid hands on everyone's head and prayed. We all need healing, and we all need prayer. The time seemed to move along somewhat quickly as Father Kelleher prayed and blessed each person. Father Kelleher approached and laid his hands on Dad's head. Unlike anyone else in the church, Father Kelleher spent an inordinate amount of time with Dad. I saw Dad cry for the first time in his life. Father Kelleher continued praying softly and powerfully in Christ as Dad wept. Our family felt something profound was happening.

Dad still had cancer, but a blessing did occur. Despite his widespread cancer and throughout the many months of his debilitating sickness, Dad felt no pain, and this freedom from pain mystified Dad's health care providers. One nurse told us it was inexplicable that despite cancer affecting so much of his body, Dad was free from pain. Although not healed, the absence of pain was a blessing for Dad.

A special hospital bed with an oxygen tank was set up in Mom and Dad's Florida living room as Dad's cancerous condition worsened dramatically. By the time I arrived from Illinois to keep watch with Mom, Dad had slipped into a coma. Mom labored with grace and courage to take care of Dad during these final, deeply sad and silent hours. One day, all of a sudden, Dad slipped out of his comatose state and looked around, his eyes darting back and forth, alert and troubled, as if suddenly awakening from a long and deep sleep. Mom and I were both excited to be able to communicate with Dad, and we immediately began talking to him. After a few short minutes, Mom asked Dad, "Do you see David?" Although my face was inches from his, Dad shook his head no. Mom then asked Dad, "Do you see Jesus?" Dad nodded yes. Within seconds Dad slipped back into his coma. The next day, as I said the Rosary, holding Dad's hand, my father suddenly ceased breathing, or so it seemed. About forty-five seconds later, there was a very deep breath. About forty-five seconds later, another very deep breath. After one more deep breath, Dad was gone.

I did not cry then, and I did not cry at Dad's funeral. About one month later, at a youth retreat, I could not stop crying. For about forty-five minutes during the Stations of the Cross, we sang a most beautiful song called "Tell the People," memorized by me still now nearly forty years later, and my tears finally flowed freely:

> Last night Jesus came to me
> Wiped the tears from my eyes
> He said not to worry,
> He would stay by my side.
>
> Tell the people I love them,
> Tell the people I care,
> When they feel far away from me,
> Tell the people I'm there.

I simply could not stop crying for nearly an hour.

Holding Dad's hand as he breathed his last was the most powerful moment of my life. Many years later as I think about Dad most every single day, it remains my most poignant memory. After the heart-changing youth retreat, I wrote a song about the experience for guitar, and although I still recall the tune, the lyrics so many years later are a little hazy yet went something like this:

> I can see your smiling face,
> I can feel your love for me.
> Whatever we would do,
> Together we would be.
> We'd go out together,
> Alone just you are me.
> Living, dreaming baseball,
> Our childhood memories.

> I held the hand of Jesus,
> As I held my father's hand.
> I love you, Dad, so dearly,
> I sure need you where I am.

> I saw you lying sick one day,
> I had to close my eyes.
> There'd be no more baseball.
> Instead of laugh, we'd cry.
> The time we had together
> Was quickly pushed aside.

Cancer racked your body,
And death was at your side.

I held the hand of Jesus,
As I held my father's hand.
I love you, Dad, so dearly,
I sure need you where I am.

Thank you for your friendship,
Thank you for your love.
Thank you for the memories,
God with you above.
The joy we shared together,
Alone just you and me.
Dad, you are my hero,
Together we will be.

I held the hand of Jesus,
As I held my father's hand.
I love you, Dad, so dearly,
I sure need you where I am.

A few years later I began my teaching and coaching career. I lived in South Minneapolis, by coincidence three blocks from where George Floyd was murdered. The year was 1992. Mom was refurnishing her Florida home and planned to buy a new recliner. Knowing how much I loved Dad, Mom did not want to get rid of Dad's old recliner and thought it would be a great gift and remembrance for me. She somehow arranged with a trucking company to ship Dad's brown La-Z-Boy recliner to me all the way from Florida to Minnesota.

I kept the recliner for the past three decades, moving with it quite often, from Minnesota to South Carolina to Virginia to Indiana and back to Virginia. As you would expect, the chair gradually became quite worn and torn. The arms became frayed and tattered, and the reclining gears broke several times. At one point more than a decade ago, the gears were so broken, the chair could not even be used at all. But a church member skilled in carpentry fixed it for me.

During the years serving at Saint Patrick's Orthodox Church, I still used Dad's old recliner. Although it was still usable, it grew more and more uncomfortable, and the gears finally broke again. Luckily the chair locked in one somewhat bearable position. One of the subdeacons at our church is quite skilled in household projects and renovations. I offered a hundred dollars to him to try to fix the gears. I told him about Dad and how the old recliner had great sentimental value for me. Yet realizing a chair half-a-century-old may soon be broken, I asked my friend to quietly toss Dad's old recliner if it was beyond repair. It simply would pass in the night as another fond but distant memory of my dad.

Nearly nine months passed and, hearing nothing, I assumed the chair was finally finished for good. Teaching fourth grade, the school year was winding down to completion. I arrived home after school one day and was greeted by what looked like a new recliner. My first thought was that Subdeacon James somehow found a different recliner for me. Yet looking more closely, this new chair actually was Dad's old recliner, completely reupholstered with fresh leather and fixed with a new gear system!

Subdeacon James had almost given up, and the chair looked like a goner for sure! But he persisted, getting help as necessary. He knew how much I loved Dad and, like anyone who has lost a parent knows, how I still think about him every day, close to forty years after holding Dad's hand on his deathbed. The chair was broken, other chairs were more comfortable and more expensive, but because it reminded me of Dad, the old recliner was priceless, a giver of precious memories.

Subdeacon James found a professional in a nearby bigger city in Northern Virginia here in the D.C. Beltway. He talked to the parish council at Saint Patrick Orthodox Church and the servers and acolytes in our Sacristy. My Dad's old recliner, with a half-century of memories, both joyful and sorrowful, is now as good as new. The gears work superbly, the old, torn leather has been completely replaced, and the chair is at its best in decades.

Mom's thoughtfulness and kindness four decades ago placed in her mind and heart the unorthodox idea of shipping an old recliner across the country to a son still missing his dad. I have called Mom each Sunday afternoon after going to church, the same time each week. I knew this story would bring great joy to her heart. When I shared with her about the kind and generous people at Saint Patrick Orthodox Church, and how Dad's old recliner was now as good as new, here is what she said: "Tell your friends at church that I really appreciate this. It's a keepsake. Tell them I appreciate it with all my heart."

So blessed to be serving as a Deacon at the best church and with the finest folks in the world.

CHAPTER TWO

JOY

(*The Word* published "The Joy of Orthodoxy"
in November-December 2020.)

"Rejoice always; pray without ceasing; in everything give thanks; for this is God's will for you in Christ Jesus" (Thessalonians 5:16-18 NASB). Joy, Prayer, Thanksgiving: these three virtuous commands both offer hope during trying times and permeate our wonder-full journey within the Orthodox Church. Our heart's response described by Saint Paul becomes a daily reality: we rejoice not occasionally but always; we pray not just on Sunday but without ceasing; our hearts overflow with gratitude. Our best friends Jesus the Christ and Mary the Theotokos reside deep down inside our hearts and guide our thoughts, words, and deeds every minute of every day.

Becoming Orthodox opens one's world to wonder like never before. "And now here is my secret, a very simple secret: It is only with the heart that one can see rightly; what is essential is invisible to the eye" (De Saint Exupéry 73). With these words, Antione de Saint-Exupéry describes the essence of seeing our world through the inner eyes of faith.

This ongoing quest for the essential and the invisible best expresses my lifelong journey into Orthodoxy.

The year is 1976, and I am a sophomore at the University of Notre Dame. Enrolled in a course entitled "Introduction to Philosophy," I expected to be challenged with the discourses of Descartes and Hume. Instead, Professor Joe Evans began our collegiate philosophical inquiry with the children's classic *The Little Prince* by Antoine de Saint-Exupéry. It was then I learned the Secret of the Fox, "that it is only with the heart that one can see rightly; what is essential is invisible to the eye" (De Saint-Exupéry 73). Fast forward thirty-six years later as His Eminence Metropolitan Kallistos Ware speaks about how to incorporate the Jesus Prayer into our daily lives at Saint Mark Coptic Orthodox Church in Fairfax, Virginia, on Saturday evening 23 June 2012. He also quoted from *The Little Prince* and later wrote to me from Oxford in Great Britain, "The book is a great favourite of mine." Citing the Secret of the Fox, Metropolitan Ware invited us to pray the Jesus Prayer for fifteen minutes each day and then spend the rest of the day loving others with Christ's love.

My journey into Orthodoxy took many unexpected twists and turns with this one great constant: The Secret of the Fox. My life has been a gradual learning of this special secret, a shift from the head to the heart, a deeper appreciation of the invisible, a journey with much joy towards "the Way and the Truth and the Life" (John 14:6 NLV).

In my own odyssey into Orthodoxy, although books took me some distance towards the truth, the Divine Liturgy has been by far the best teacher. In this regard, the Divine Liturgy emphasizes the great mysteries from the Annunciation to Pentecost surrounding the miraculous manifestation of Jesus Christ our Saviour. The Divine Liturgy presents an amazing array of special feast days while being itself each time we go to church an indescribably magnificent feast. "Feast means joy" (Schmemann, *For the Life of the World* 63 (emphasis in original)). The Divine Liturgy experienced as "heaven on earth" best exemplifies this unbounded joy and serves as the most constant anchor of our lives. "Our Church remains a liturgical Church par excellence not only in the sense of the uninterruptedness of her ancient tradition of worship, but also because of the place which worship occupies in the life of the faithful, because of the special love the faithful have for the church building and its services" (Schmemann, *Introduction to Liturgical Theology* 27). We experience the pinnacle of Orthodoxy during the celebration of the Divine Liturgy.

Notre Dame Professor Joe Evans used to tell us, "No wonder, no philosophy... and no wonder!" Wonder erupts anew during the Divine Liturgy. As we kneel during the Western Rite Canon of the Mass at Saint Patrick Orthodox Church, as the priest boldly recreates the words of Christ at the Last Supper, "Take, eat; this is My body... Drink from it, all of you. For this is My blood" (Matthew 26:26-27 NKJV), we witness with our own eyes the greatest miracle we could ever ask or imagine. Minutes later during our Mass, as we eat His Body and drink His Blood, we live totally and completely in communion with Christ. "He that eateth my flesh, and drinketh my blood, dwelleth in me, and I in him" (John 6:56 KJV).

"The sting of death is sin, and the power of sin is the law; but thanks be to God, who gives us the victory through our Lord Jesus Christ" (1 Thessalonians 5:16-18 NASB). How soon we forget this heavenly victory! As we leave the church parking lot, do our minds begin shifting away from the inner joy and peace of the Mass? As we drive to work on Monday morning, has the Eucharistic miracle receded from our hearts? Our lives seem surprisingly ordinary given the profound Eucharistic miracle we experience every time we receive Holy Communion. How strong is the joyful wonder of Holy Communion in our lives? How do we maintain and nurture this joyful wonder in our minds and hearts? How can we carry this joyful wonder with us into our homes and work places throughout the whole week? How can we bring this joyful wonder to the forefront of our everyday lives, every minute of every day?

The answer lies in Saint Paul's simple command: "Rejoice always, pray without ceasing; in everything give thanks; for this is God's will for you in Christ Jesus" (1 Thessalonians 5:16-18 NASB). With joyful hearts filled with thanksgiving, we remember our Holy Communion often and in so doing fulfill God's most holy will for our lives. We embrace the deepest experiential aspect of our Orthodox faith, the reception of the Holy Eucharist, with a conscious decision to continually pray, with joy and thanks, deepening our eternal friendships with Jesus the Christ and Mary the Theotokos every minute of every day. Orthodoxy fills our minds and hearts with joyful wonder.

BIBLIOGRAPHY

De Saint-Exupéry, Antoine. *The Little Prince*. San Diego: Harcourt Brace, 1971.

Schmemann, Alexander. *For the Life of the World*. Crestwood, NY: St. Vladimir's Seminary Press, 1973.

Schmemann, Alexander. *Introduction to Liturgical Theology*. Crestwood, NY: St. Vladimir's Seminary Press, 2003.

CHAPTER THREE

PEACE

(*The Word* published "The Rocky Mountain Monastery" in May-June 2022.)

"And now here is a secret, a very simple secret: It is only with the heart that one can see rightly; what is essential is invisible to the eye" (de Saint-Exupéry 73). With these words, Antoine de Saint-Exupéry describes the essence of seeing our world through the inner eyes of faith. This lifelong quest for the essential and invisible beauty of our lives in Christ best expresses two pre-pandemic summer visits to the magnificent Monastery of Our Lady and Saint Laurence in the Rocky Mountains of Colorado.

THE JOURNEY

Most drive yet some fly to visit the Mountain Monastery. I began my two trips to Colorado from Saint Patrick Orthodox Church in Virginia. Baptized as an infant, I never really looked closely at my Baptismal Certificate issued shortly after my birth until a few years after being chrismated into to Orthodox Church on the Feast of the Nativity of the Blessed

Virgin Mary on Sunday 8 September 2013. Amazing how God works in all our lives. Mom and Dad met at Marshall Field's in downtown Chicago after World War Two. A tall, handsome man, Dad served as a Lieutenant at Guadalcanal and became a Lieutenant Colonel in the Army. Mom was a rare beauty with spark, smarts, and wit. Blessed beyond measure to be their youngest son, I was born nearly a decade later in Valparaiso, Indiana, and baptized as an infant at Saint Patrick Catholic Church in nearby Chesterton. More than fifty years later, I was chrismated at Saint Patrick Orthodox Church in Virginia. All our lifelong journeys are in similar ways strikingly orchestrated by the hand of Almighty God.

The cross-country trek across our spacious land is magnificent. Driving through the Appalachian Mountains in the East toward the Rocky Mountains in the West, you travel through the flatlands of Iowa and Nebraska. While tourists visit Europe for the history, art, and architecture, a drive across America is filled with natural wonders. Whether you travel to the Monastery of Our Lady and Saint Laurence by land or by air, the last dozen miles are the same for everyone as you leave the paved highway to traverse the bumpy dirt road upward toward the monastery. A prayerful retreat both slows your pace and clears your mind, and this last leg of your journey with winding curves and dusty roads launches the quieting of your soul.

Tired from your long journey, you step from your car and immediately find yourself mesmerized by the scenery. The Rocky Mountains embrace you with their immense beauty. "The world is charged with the grandeur of God" (Hopkins 66). A steep mountain cliff rising upward on your left, two layers of mountaintops in front of you and to your right, all topped with a Virgin Mary blue sky with pristine white clouds. An artist's heaven, a poet's paradise.

THE CHURCH

Heaven on earth, all day and all night. Lauds before dawn, Sacred Scripture sung and spoken methodically and carefully. Slowly and precisely, each word becomes a Word of God to be prayed in faith, from the heart, deep down inside. You pause in the middle of each verse, thinking "Jesus, Jesus" with an intake of air before finishing. The Western Rite Mass soon follows with mostly hidden yet partially revealed mysteries touching our feeble minds and burdened hearts. The ancient Divine Liturgy of Saint Gregory the Great is filled with sublime beauty. The Epistle and Gospel, the magnificent Canon of the Mass, the Body and Blood of Christ, the priest's Blessing. Lord, we truly are not worthy. Immersed in holiness, time flies, the service completed in the blink of an eye.

"Pray without ceasing" (1 Thessalonians 5:17 NKJV). In a monastery, the monks pray… and pray and pray and pray! They pray in the church, through their chores, at their rest, during their sleep. "Seven times a day do I praise thee because of thy righteous judgments" (Psalm 119:164 KJV). We see Prime, Lauds, Terce, Sext, None, Vespers, and Compline. This is only the beginning.

Compline is quiet and simple, profound and powerful. Before it begins, the monks ask for mutual forgiveness. At the end, a beautiful rendition of the *Salve Regina* is accompanied by a procession to the back side altar of Our Lady of Glastonbury. Among the saints in the icon of Our Lady, I see Saint Joseph of Arimathea and am reminded of Metropolitan Joseph. I see Saint Patrick and am reminded of the wonder-filled folks from my home parish in Virginia. I see Saint Dunstan, a blacksmith holding the tools of his trade and a chalice, and I am reminded of Father Patrick, our parish priest, laboring at his blacksmith shop and raising the chalice during the Canon of the Mass.

My favourite time of the day during my monastery visits occurred immediately after Compline. As the Grand Silence descends, a door opens in the heart. For nearly four decades, I discovered immense joy and peace while slowly pacing inside large churches. In old churches, I ponder the hundreds of thousands of prayers lifted towards heaven by our faithful, fallen-asleep people in the pews. In new churches, I marvel at the precious beauty of the icons and the architectural magnificence of the pillars and high ceilings. Within the monastery church, facing the East, I walk slowly towards the giant golden Crucifix, the icons of Madonna and Child and the Risen Christ, the glass Tabernacle containing the Corpus Christi, and the altar relics of the Blessed Virgin Mary on the left and Saint Benedict on the right. Taking a step towards the South, I see the large icons of Saint Benedict, Saint Bede, and Saint Antony. Turning the corner to walk toward the West, in the back of church, I pause in deep respect and admiration before some of the greatest heroes of our timeless Orthodox tradition, in order from left to right: Saint Peter the Apostle, Saint Ambrose, Saint Augustine, Saint Jerome, Saint Gregory the Great, Our Lady of Glastonbury, Saint Gregory the Theologian, Saint Basil the Great, Saint John Chrysostom, Saint Athanasius, and Saint Paul the Apostle. Turning to finish the square by slowly pacing towards the North, I recognize the beauty of Saint Cecilia, Saint Agnes of Rome, and Saint Katharine. A slow walk around the church to calm the human heart and experience the divine presence. I leave the church for my cell in the dark of night filled with awe and wonder and ready to sleep in joy and peace.

COME AND SEE

You cannot adequately describe the Orthodox Church in words. The best you can say to both friend and stranger searching for truth and looking for love is, "Come and see." The best vacation you and your family can take during the summer of 2022 is to "come and see" the Mountain Monastery in Colorado. Your life will be changed forever.

Surrounded by God's grandeur and touched by God's grace, you also will be embraced by the heartfelt warmth of monastic hospitality. Driving up the winding dirt road and passing through the gate, you may see deer or elk, rattlesnake or chipmunk, and even an occasional mountain lion or bear. Once you arrive at Our Lady and Saint Laurence Monastery, Dom Theodore will greet you with a smile and a hug, and in your heart you will realize you truly have come home.

BIBLIOGRAPHY

De Saint-Exupéry, Antoine. *The Little Prince*. San Diego: Harcourt Brace, 1971.

Hopkins, Gerard Manley. *The Poems of Gerard Manley Hopkins*, ed. W. H. Gardner & N. H. Mackenzie. London: Oxford University Press, 1967.

CHAPTER FOUR

LONGSUFFERING

Every time there is another school shooting in America, our nation shudders. Some call for more security, with more law enforcement officers protecting our children within their schools. Others suggest arming teachers. Still others call for the elimination of certain weapons. Many folks hurting inside after witnessing on television the suffering of our children immediately turn their hearts towards God in humble prayer and supplication.

Some believe gun violence in America can be solved legislatively. Others seek a spiritual solution. Isn't it true our only long-lasting hope of ending school shootings involves turning our hearts and hopefully our nation towards God?

Evil is the absence of good, not something lurking out there, outside of ourselves. We begin our journey by delving deeply into our own hearts to discover what separates us from the goodness of God. "Wash yourselves, make yourselves clean; Put away the evil of your doings from before My eyes" (Isaiah 1:16 NKJV). Only after striving to discard the powerful influence of sin in our own hearts will we be able to reach towards the good:

Learn to do good;
Seek justice,
Rebuke the oppressor;
Defend the fatherless,
Plead for the widow (Isaiah 1:17 NKJV).

Meaningful solutions to eradicating gun violence begin at home, within our own hearts and minds.

One thing seems crystal clear. "I am the vine, you are the branches; the one who remains in Me, and I in him bears much fruit, for apart from Me you can do nothing" (John 15:5 NASB). We cannot find a solution on our own. Proposals to curtail school violence in America are destined to fail unless the power and presence of God are brought to the forefront. We need help. Our nation desperately needs God.

"Come now, and let us reason together,"
Says the LORD,
"Though your sins are like scarlet,
They shall be as white as snow;
Though they are red like crimson,
They shall be as wool" (Isaiah 1:18 NKJV).

Humility before the face of God is an essential starting point in trying to find solutions to every single problem present in the world today.

The Prophet Isaiah calls us to a willing obedience. The Lawgiver Moses put this in even starker terms: choose life and good by rejecting death and evil:

> See, I have set before you today life and good, death and evil, in that I command you today to love the Lord your God, to walk in His ways, and to keep His commandments, His statutes, and His judgments, that you may live and multiply; and the Lord your God will bless you in the land which you go to possess. But if your heart turns away so that you do not hear, and are drawn away, and worship other gods and serve them, I announce to you today that you shall surely perish (Deuteronomy 30:15-18a NKJV).

Isn't there a sense of heavy angst and oppressive fear within our hearts telling us that things in our nation just aren't right?

The Orthodox Church offers both immense insight and practical solutions to our nation and world during these troubling times. Our Divine Liturgies, the source of our rich theology, offer the best hope.

One of the children at our church recently asked me, "What is your favourite part of Holy Week?" Two images readily came to heart and mind: the Word of God and the Bread of Life. My favourite singular event during Holy Week occurred during the reading of the twelve Old Testament prophecies at Pascha. These powerful proclamations specifically selected by the Church for this special liturgical time evoked an hour of deep reflection encompassing almost a third of our lengthy worship. Similarly, my favourite evening Mass occurred during the celebration of Maundy Thursday as we recalled the institution of the Holy Eucharist, the life-giving, miraculous gift of the Body and Blood of

Christ. Both God's Holy Word and Christ's Holy Eucharist surround and engulf us within the Trinitarian Presence of Father, Son, and Holy Spirit, providing the greatest source of our hope for a better tomorrow.

During the Old Testament readings from Pascha, we prayed and pondered together in a candlelit church being embraced by the most magnificent stories from our rich salvation history described in the Old Testament. Through these readings, we also catch a glimpse of the human heart and our lifelong battle against sin. Creatures Adam and Eve rebelled against their Uncreated God, choosing their own will rather than following the will of their Creator. Humanity became so depraved in our pursuit of evil, substituting our own way for God's infinitely better plan for us, that an historic flood destroyed nearly all of the human race. God called Abram, and Abraham demonstrated His love for God by being willing to sacrifice his beloved son, trusting Isaac would be raised from the dead. Moses met God at the burning bush, standing upon holy ground like we rise together at church, and God miraculously parted the Red Sea so His chosen people could escape from slavery into freedom. The dry bones sprung to new life; a man emerged from the belly of a whale after three days. Magnificent recollections poignantly and powerfully directed our hearts and minds towards the death and resurrection of Jesus.

These Old Testament readings express the Liturgy of the Word. Even more beloved for me personally, the Liturgy of the Eucharist brought to fruition during the Last Supper and celebrated on Maundy Thursday elicits both mystery and wonder. "The sacred Altar is the focal point of the worshipping congregation, because there the Sacrament of the divine Eucharist is celebrated. The fact that the Book of the Gospels lies upon it demonstrates the connection between Holy Scripture and worship."[1] Receiving the Eucharist, consuming the actual Body and Blood of Christ, opens an infinite, ever-expanding universe of possibilities into our lives and our world. "He who eats My flesh and drinks My blood abides in Me, and I in him" (John 6:56 NKJV).

Taught by Sacred Scriptures and nourished by the Body and Blood of Christ, our Orthodox Church stands in a unique position to offer the very best hope and the most practical solutions to the woes of the world. The Eucharist stands as the "source and goal of the entire liturgical life of the Church."[2] To understand this, we must contemplate the rich reality of the Real Presence of Jesus Christ and hence the Trinity within the Eucharist. "I believe and I confess that for the Church, for the world, for mankind there is no more important, more urgent question than *what is accomplished in the eucharist*."[3] During every single Divine Liturgy, we witness a magnificent miracle. The priest in the person of Christ offers the bread and wine and, miraculously, these common staples of life become the Body and Blood of Christ. The bread and wine in the Eucharist are truly

---

[1] Metropolitan of Nafpaktos Hierotheos, *Hesychia and Theology: The Context for Man's Healing in the Orthodox Church*, translated by Sister Pelagia Selfe (Levadia, Greece: Birth of the Theotokos Monastery, 2007), 181.

[2] Alexander Schmemann, *Introduction to Liturgical Theology* (Crestwood, NY: St. Vladimir's Seminary Press, 2003), 24.

[3] Alexander Schmemann, *The Eucharist* (Crestwood, NY: St. Vladimir's Seminary Press, 1987), 163 (emphasis in original).

"the Body and Blood of Christ, His *parousia*, His presence among us."[4] We later consume the Body and Blood of our crucified and risen Lord, the Second Person of the Trinity. "Through the sacrament of the Holy Eucharist, God enters into union with the whole man."[5] Blessed beyond more than we can ask or imagine, "Through the Holy Eucharist, we are transformed into that which we receive."[6]

Our transformation is trinitarian. "God has chosen us not for death, but for life, whose *telos* or ultimate goal is eternal communion with the Persons of the Holy Trinity."[7] When we receive the Body and Blood of Christ during the Divine Liturgy, our hearts are filled with the power and presence of God the Father, God the Son, and God the Holy Spirit. "Being offered in the Son, it is offered to the Father. Being offered to the Father, it is fulfilled in the partaking of the Holy Spirit. And therefore the eucharist is the eternally living and lifecreating source of the Church's knowledge of the Most Holy Trinity."[8] God the Father, God the Son, and God the Holy Ghost are never divided, never apart. "This acceptance of the Son, this union in him with the Father, is fulfilled as salvation, as the new life, as the kingdom of God in the communion of the Holy Spirit, which is the divine

---

[4] Alexander Schmemann, *Of Water & the Spirit* (Crestwood, New York: St. Vladimir's Seminary Press, 1974), 50.

[5] Joseph Allen, *And He Leads Them* (Ben Lomond, CA: Conciliar Press, 2001), 93.

[6] Christoforos Stavropouplos, *Partakers of Divine Nature* (Minneapolis, MN: Light and Life Publishing, 1976), 59.

[7] John Breck, *The Sacred Gift of Life* (Crestwood, New York: St. Vladimir's Seminary Press, 1998), 215.

[8] Alexander Schmemann, *The Eucharist*, 167.

life itself, communion with God. And thus, the eucharist is also the sacrament of our *access* to God and knowledge of him and union with him."[9]

Our society is sick in so many ways. School shootings don't just emerge from within a vacuum. Our young people committing these horrendous atrocities grow up in a world of moral relativism where subjective wants and desires replace objective truth and science. Our children are taught to place themselves at the center of the universe and to define their own unique truths. Society bombards our children with violent images and practices that poison their souls.

We all find ourselves in need of healing, and our Church truly is a hospital for sinners. Only by immersing our young people in the liturgical life of the Church will their souls be healed and the violence actions of a sickened soul cease.

Imagine a world where our young people learn the value of immersing themselves in the still silence of the Divine Liturgy and becoming united to our Almighty Creator in an indescribable way beyond human comprehension. "As we partake of His human Body and Blood we receive God Himself into our souls. It is thus God's Body and Blood which we receive, His soul, mind, and will, no less than those of His humanity."[10] Our humanity touches God's divinity. A young person whose heart and mind touches God's

---

[9] Ibid (emphasis in original).
[10] Nicholas Cabasilas, *The Life in Christ*, translated by Carmino J. deCatanzaro (Crestwood, NY: St. Vladimir's Seminary Press, 1974), 122.

divinity will not kill his classmates. This and this alone is the only sure solution to the plethora of school shootings plaguing and permeating our great land.

The best answer to tackling all our social problems is found in a deep and abiding union and communion with our Lord and Saviour Jesus Christ. "A man is returned to that place that God had prepared for him when he created the world. He stands at the heights, before the throne of God; he stands in heaven, before the face of God himself, and freely, in the fulness of love and knowledge, uniting in himself the whole world, all creation, he offers thanksgiving, and in him the whole world affirms and acknowledges this thanksgiving to be 'meet and right.' This man is Christ. He alone is without sin, he alone is Man in all the fulness of his purpose, calling and glory."[11] Introducing our young people to the love of the Holy Trinity is the answer.

As we reflect on the potent pain and horrendous hurt afflicting our nation because of school shootings, begin first with prayer and in humility beg for God's mercy. Recognize our own sinfulness and falling away from grace. And then think about Holy Communion. Saint Ignatius of Antioch describes the Eucharist as a medicine for our immorality or new life in Christ.[12] God created our human nature to share in His divine nature, and the best expressions of this union and communion with God occur when we read God's Word and receive Holy Communion.

---

[11] Alexander Schmemann, *The Eucharist*, 170.
[12] Ibid., 109.

According as his divine power hath given unto us all things that pertain unto life and godliness, through the knowledge of him that hath called us to glory and virtue: Whereby are given unto us exceeding great and precious promises: that by these ye might be partakers of the divine nature, having escaped the corruption that is in the world through lust (2 Peter 1:3-4 KJV).

We must spread the Joy of Orthodoxy across our nation, showing our young people the Way, inspiring them with the Truth, and sharing with them our Life in Christ.

CHAPTER FIVE

KINDNESS

For now we see in a mirror, dimly, but then face to face. Now I know in part, but then I shall know just as I also am known (1 Corinthians 13:12 NKJV).

Mom celebrated her one hundredth birthday in the early days of August. She recently called me one morning in the midst of a busy school day. Teachers are not allowed to take personal calls at school, but even in the middle of a lecture, when you see there is a telephone call from your one-hundred-year-old mother, you pick up.

Upon receiving my first short book in the mail, Mom read *Prayers to Our Lady East and West* three times already. With Mom on the telephone and me standing in front of seventeen fourth graders, a brilliant idea popped into my head through God's grace, and I suggested to the children, "Hey, everybody, let's all sing 'Happy Birthday' to my mom. She just turned one hundred years old this summer!"

The children sang enthusiastically with both godly grace and poignant beauty. Their impromptu musical presentation deeply touched Mom's heart.

Following a family tradition begun nearly two decades ago, I call Mom on the telephone every Sunday afternoon after church at precisely the same time each week. As we talked about the fourth-grade birthday song one afternoon, still much moved, Mom began to cry. As told to me by a wise priest many years ago, I shared with Mom the profound truth, "Tears are a gift from God."

Travel back in time with me more than one hundred fifty years.

A baby is born on the 21st day of January in 1869 at Mariampol, Lithuania. Bonifacius and Alena name their oldest son Vincent William, and growing up in his homeland across the ocean, young Vincent nurtures a dream deep within his heart. He longs to travel to the United States of America.

The French gave "The Statue of Liberty Enlightening the World" to the United States as a sign of friendship, and the magnificent statue in New York City was dedicated by President Grover Cleveland on the 28th day of October in 1886. Grandpa was seventeen years old. That very same year, according to an edition of *Who's Who in Chicago* from the 1930's, Grandpa emigrated from Lithuania to the United States. He may have seen the Statue of Liberty from the ship. Because he did not understand any English at the time, young Vincent could not have read and understood the words inscribed upon the statue's base, the conclusion of a sonnet entitled "The New Colossus" composed by Emma Lazarus in 1883:

> Give me your tired, your poor,
> Your huddled masses yearning to breathe free,
> The wretched refuse of your teeming shore.

> Send these, the homeless, tempest-tost to me,
> I lift my lamp beside the golden door!

Naturalized in 1896, Vincent became a citizen of the United States of America on the 11th day of March in 1899 at the age of thirty in Green Bay, Wisconsin. Grandpa learned to speak the English language and, with much grit and hard work, graduated from law school and became a successful Chicago attorney.

Grandpa was fifty years old when he met and married his wife Mamie, twenty years younger than himself. Mom was born when her father was fifty-three years old. As Mom recalls the family history one century later, she recently during our weekly call shared how Grandpa actually travelled across the Atlantic Ocean with only sixteen cents in his pocket. Just prior to the Stock Market Crash of 1929, during which he lost a small fortune, Grandpa was recognized as one of the top lawyers of Lithuanian descent. Married and raising a young daughter during the Great Depression, Grandpa worked hard as an attorney to rebuild his wealth, starting again from scratch after losing everything during the Great Crash.

According to Grandma during one of our long talks at night during my college years, whereas her own special interests were her grandchildren and writing letters, Grandpa's chief interest was "romping with his daughter." Mom, a gifted only child, skillfully played both the violin and the family's Mason & Hamlin Grand Piano at the age of six. She arrived at Saint Rita Grammar School already knowing how to read, and was so smart, the sisters promoted her immediately from first to fourth grade. She walked down the hall at age six to read *Treasure Island* to the eighth graders. Later in the upper grades, Mom played the piano from the third floor at Saint Rita as the students marched from school. A wonder-filled mother and accomplished career woman, Mom graduated from high school at the age of fifteen and the Art Institute with a Bachelor of Fine Arts through the University of Chicago at nineteen. She met Dad, a United States Army Colonel, after World War Two at Marshall Field's in downtown Chicago. They lived in a Frank Lloyd Wright house early in their marriage, and after four children were born, my family settled in Fort Wayne, Indiana, my childhood hometown.

I spoke with Mom Sunday after church a few weeks following the children's superb singing of "Happy Birthday." Their beautiful voices truly touched her heart. She shared, "I listen to it in my head all the time." Amazing how one single act of kindness by a fourth-grade classroom can bring joy and hope beyond the moment, creating a powerful and moving memory to last a lifetime.

Another beautiful event happened recently.

Right next door to where Mom resides at Luther Manor, her independent living apartment complex in Wauwatosa, Wisconsin, stands an historic edifice, Annunciation Greek Orthodox Church. The church was designed by the famous American architect Frank Lloyd Wright in 1956 with construction completed in 1961. Listed on the National Register of Historic Places, it is one of my two church homes-away-from-home while travelling during each summer vacation from school to visit my family up North. This August, for example, I celebrated the Feast of the Transfiguration at Annunciation Greek Orthodox Church in Wisconsin on Saturday and worshipped with Father Peter Jon and his mother Khouria Marilyn at All Saints Orthodox Church in Indiana on Sunday.

I first met Father Ciprian, the Greek Orthodox priest at Annunciation, more than a year ago. I visited his church one summer Sunday, and he and his family, like his predecessor at the church Father John, were exceptionally hospitable. It brought great joy to my heart to be allowed to stand behind the templon to the side as a guest, rejoicing in my heart to be so close to the miraculous action at the Holy Altar. The magnificent beauty of the Eastern Orthodox Divine Liturgy was brought to life as Father Ciprian celebrated with Father Aurel, his father from Romania, at his side. Presvytera Magdalena, Father Ciprian's wonder-full wife, led the chanting of the choir.

Nearly two months after Mom's one-hundredth birthday party, I was surprised to receive a private message from Father Ciprian. He just received a signed copy of *Prayers to Our Lady East and West* in the mail and wrote, "Thank you for the kind gift of the book. I want to touch base with you about your mother as I'd like to visit her today or tomorrow." These kind words launched an array of amazing adventures.

My fourth graders began praying in earnest that Father Ciprian and Mom actually would connect, and our Blessed Lord answered their powerful prayers. Mom's independent living complex is huge. Visiting Mom during my summer vacation for years, I found myself lost many a time, as the differently-lettered levels and hallways remind me of a mouse's maze. Similarly, the Lord saw fit that Father Ciprian be blessed that day with a very long walk between many different buildings, trying numerous different intercoms and talking with random people for more directions; meanwhile, Mom walked up and down her hallway calling his name. Eventually they met and enjoyed a good laugh together as they talked about the adventurous search prior to their first meeting. Father Ciprian let me know, "After I left your mom's apartment, I still had a smile on my face, as I was taking my long walk back to my office."

Within my heart, the one word best describing our Uncreated God of Infinite Love is *mystery*. The rich theology within the Eastern Orthodox Church both East and West is united and one. Our approach to worship, both Eastern Rite and Western Rite, magnifies the timeless transcendence of Almighty God. Although there are many similarities between our respective church calendars in our Eastern and Western traditions, some differences exist. Rather than a liability, this diversity based upon centuries of historical events and cultural circumstances is a most beautiful blessing. God works mysteriously throughout this tapestry of our rich, shared tradition.

Father Ciprian's first meeting with Mom occurred on Tuesday the 11th day of October. At Saint Patrick Orthodox Church in Virginia, my Western Rite parish, we joyfully worshipped God with a High Solemn Mass that evening by celebrating the Feast of the Motherhood of the Blessed Virgin Mary. Although this particular feast day is not shared by our Eastern Rite brothers and sisters, an enthusiastic and energetic Greek Orthodox priest blessed my mother, a lifelong Roman Catholic, during this ancient and uniquely Western feast honouring the Motherhood of the Blessed Virgin Mary, the Theotokos, the Mother of God.

During my yearly visit to Annunciation Greek Orthodox Church in August, one short day after Mom's surprise hundredth birthday party, I met Father Ciprian's wife Presvytera Magdalena after the Divine Liturgy during which she beautifully led the chants. Near the front steps of the church, Maggie pointed to a building across the way where Father Ciprian's beloved mother lived during her last months on earth when she could no longer attend the Divine Liturgy because of her illness. Unable to be present in person, Presvytera Lidia waited by the window to see her family wave from the front steps of the church before and after the Divine Liturgy prior to their family gathering. Presvytera Lidia fell asleep on the 25th day of September in 2021.

My Sunday afternoon talks with Mom, a continual source of inspiration infused with a century of rich family memories, received an added spiritual blessing since Mom's first meeting with Father Ciprian. Our immortal and infinite God embraces our lives in hidden, silent ways far beyond our limited ability to even begin to understand. I praise God because Mom and Dad made sure I was baptized as an infant at Saint Patrick Catholic Church in Chesterton, Indiana. I rejoice that more than six decades later, I serve as a deacon at Saint Patrick Orthodox Church in Bealeton, Virginia.

During her century on earth, Mom loved two priests in particular, Father Edward and Father James, both of blessed memory, during my formative Indiana years attending Saint

Charles Borromeo School, Bishop Dwenger High School, and the University of Notre Dame. Mom joyfully related during a recent Sunday afternoon talk that Father Ciprian was the very first priest ever to greet her with a hug! She also marveled how Father Ciprian took the time to wear his special vestments to anoint her with holy oil during their visit.

This prayerful priestly encounter brought an abundance of joy and hope to Mom. Father Ciprian wrote, "Your mom is an amazing woman full of life who, in my opinion, looks only half her age. I can't wait for my wife Maggie to meet her too."

I mentioned to Mom that Father Ciprian lost his own mother to illness last year. My one-hundred-year-old Mom quickly and quietly responded, "I can be his mother."

CHAPTER SIX

GOODNESS

(*The Word* published "Our Lady East and West"
in May-June 2021.)

"More honourable than the Cherubim, and beyond compare more glorious than the Seraphim, thee who without corruption gavest birth to God the Word, the very Theotokos, thee do we magnify."[13] These words of veneration for the Blessed Virgin Mary, prayed and sung throughout the Orthodox Church for centuries, epitomize the special love relationship between the Theotokos and the Orthodox faithful.

"Throughout history, and especially during the fourth and fifth centuries, the basic category for thinking about Mary was that of paradox: Virgin and Mother; Human Mother of One who is God, Theotokos."[14] A theological understanding of Our Lady is found most readily in the Divine Liturgy. "In

---

[13] Holy Transfiguration Monastery, trans., *The Service of the Akathist Hymn: The Salutations to the Most Holy Theotokos* (Boston, MA: Holy Transfiguration Monastery, 1991), 79.

[14] Jaroslav Pelikan, *Mary Through the Centuries* (New Haven and London: Yale University Press, 1996), 55.

Orthodox services Mary is often mentioned, and on each occasion she is usually given her full title: 'Our All-Holy, immaculate, most blessed and glorified Lady, Mother of God and Ever-Virgin Mary.' Here are included the three chief epithets applied to Our Lady by the Orthodox Church: *Theotokos* (God-bearer, Mother of God), *Aeiparthenos* (Ever-Virgin), and *Panagia* (All-Holy)."[15] The veracity of these titles for the Blessed Virgin Mary has been affirmed throughout church history, especially in the ecumenical councils. "The authority for these epithets is to be found in the records of the early ecumenical councils."[16] The veneration of Our Lady permeates the life of the Orthodox Church. "Although these titles have never been defined explicitly in an ecumenical council of the Eastern Orthodox Churches, they are used frequently in liturgy and personal prayer."[17] Every Orthodox Church features an icon of the Virgin Mary and the Child Jesus near the altar, and our people's intense love for the Theotokos runs wide and deep. These three titles of the Virgin Mary will be considered in turn.

The Virgin Mary is called the Theotokos or God-bearer from the earliest centuries of the Orthodox faith. Around the year 250 A.D., the term *Theotokos* "was found in a prayer written on a fragment of Egyptian papyrus for use during

....

[15] Bishop Kallistos Ware, *The Orthodox Church* (London: Penguin Books, 1997), 257-258.

[16] Andrew Louth, "John of Damascus on the Mother of God as a Link Between Humanity and God," Chap. 10 in *The Cult of the Mother of God in Byzantium,* ed. Leslie Brubaker and Mary Cunningham (Burlington, VT: Ashgate Publishing, 2011), 154.

[17] Mary Christine Athans, *In Quest of the Jewish Mary* (Maryknoll, NY: Orbis Books, 2013), 27.

the Coptic Nativity Liturgy. The prayer is known as the *Sub Tuum Praesidium* (translated into English as, "Beneath Thy Compassion"). The significance of the use of this written word in this prayer indicates that it was in common use during this liturgy and most likely used at least decades prior."[18] In addition, as most likely the oral tradition precedes the written word, it is likely the figure of the Virgin Mary was venerated quite early in church history. "Precisely because the Son of God became incarnate in Mary's womb, she is rightly called Mother of God."[19]

Mary also is referred to as *Aeiparthenos*, the Ever-Virgin. "Turning to the Fathers, one of the first proclamations of the doctrine of the virginal conception is by Ignatius of Antioch,"[20] a saint and bishop living in the first and second centuries. St. Ambrose (340-397) "appreciated how hard it was to maintain Christian virginity, and so he offered Mary as a companion to the celibates who tried. The purity of her body and her decorous comportment were to be emulated by women who strove for virtue, since Mary was a mirror of all virtues."[21] Mary as Ever-Virgin cleanses those mired in sin and striving for holiness: "O Pure One without flaw,

---

[18] Andrew Gary Podolak, "*Most Holy Theotokos, Save Us*," Master's thesis, Balamand University, 2015, 12.

[19] Luigi Gambero, *Mary and the Fathers of the Church: The Blessed Virgin Mary in Patristic Thought* (San Francisco: Ignatius Press, 1999), 153.

[20] Brian K. Reynolds, *Gateway to Heaven: Marian Doctrine and Devotion Image and Typology in the Patristic and Medieval Period*, vol. 1 (Hyde Park, NY: New City Press, 2012), 54.

[21] Miri Rubin, *Mother of God: A History of the Virgin Mary* (New Haven & London: Yale University Press, 2009), 27.

Holy One without blemish, Cleanse me that I might become pure. Sanctify me and I shall be made holy."[22] The Virgin Mary inspires all Orthodox Christians, both celibate and married, to faithfully live their respective holy callings in purity and chastity. "Blessed is she who received the Holy Spirit; He purified and polished her, and He made her a temple, and the Lord Most High dwelt in her abode."[23] Mary's virginity makes her uniqueness as the Mother of God even more pronounced, as only a pure and holy woman would be able to bear the Son of God in her virginal womb.

Besides being the Mother of God and pure virgin, Mary is called *Panagia*, the All-Holy. "Mary became 'all holy' as a result of the process of *theosis* (deification or divinization), and this was the result of both 'her free will and consent and … of the grace of the Logos of God.'"[24] After Mary assents to become the Mother of Jesus, the Holy Spirit "sanctified her, purified her and made her blessed among women… She was summoned that she might be the Mother of the Son of God; the Holy Spirit had sanctified her and so dwelt within her."[25] How was Mary, born of a man and a woman, able to overcome the corruption of the human propensity to sin? "The

....

[22] John Anthony McGuckin, *The Harp of Glory: Enzira Sebhat* (Yonkers, NY: St. Vladimir's Seminary Press, 2010), 63.

[23] Jacob of Serug, *On the Mother of God* (Crestwood, NY: St. Vladimir's Seminary Press, 1998), 41.

[24] Fastiggi, Robert L., "The Immaculate Conception: Historical and Ecumenical Perspectives," in *De Maria Numquam Satis: The Significance of the Catholic Doctrines on the Blessed Virgin Mary*, ed. Judith Marie Gentle and Robert L. Fastiggi, 1-16 (Lanham, MD: University Press of America, 2009), 9.

[25] Jacob of Serug, *On the Mother of God*, 34.

Son of God wanted to be related to her, and first He made her body without sin."[26] The glorification of Mary resounds from the angelic hosts in heaven: "The heavenly company performed their 'Holy, Holy, Holy,' unto the glorious soul of this Mother of the Son of God."[27]

St. Ambrose "places his Mariology firmly within the Christological context."[28] Specifically, for St. Ambrose, "the Virgin Birth is closely related to the divinity of Christ." [29] Mary's status within the Orthodox Church exists primarily because of her pivotal role in the mystery of the Incarnation. "Anyone who thinks out the implications of that great phrase, *The Word was made flesh*, cannot but feel a profound awe for her who was chosen as the instrument of so surpassing a mystery."[30] The essence of the Incarnation is remembered and recited at the end of every Western Rite Mass, as the priest reads about the Incarnation of Jesus from John 1:1-14 in the Last Gospel after the Final Blessing of the people. In addition, just prior to the singing of the closing recessional hymn, the priest and people pray the Angelus together. The Theotokos is immersed in the mystery of the Incarnation, next to the Trinity the most profound mystery of our faith. "She gave flesh to her Son, and she is this God-bearing and theophoric flesh through which the flesh

....

[26] Ibid., 35.

[27] Ibid., 98.

[28] Hilda Graef, *Mary: A History of Doctrine and Devotion*, vol. 1 (New York: Sheed and Ward, 1963), 78.

[29] Ibid., 79.

[30] Ware, *The Orthodox Church*, 258.

of the world is brought to Him for salvation."[31] Her unique role in the Incarnation is both essential and indispensable.

Two beautiful devotional prayers from both the East and the West honour and venerate the Theotokos, the Blessed Virgin Mary: *The Prayer Rule of the Theotokos* in the East and the Rosary in the West. At the heart of each prayer, a special tribute to Our Lady is spoken most often. First, from *The Prayer Rule of the Theotokos*, the following prayer to the Theotokos is said: "Rejoice, O Virgin Theotokos Mary, full of grace, the Lord is with You. Blessed are you among women, and blessed is the fruit of Your womb, for you have born Christ, the Savior of our souls."[32] Second, the "centerpiece of the Rosary"[33] is the Hail Mary: "Hail Mary, full of grace. The Lord is with thee. Blessed art thou among women, and blessed is the fruit of thy womb, Jesus. Holy Mary, Mother of God, pray for us sinners, now and at the hour of our death. Amen."[34] Our diverse and wonderful Orthodox Church is doubly blessed by our mutual heartfelt devotion to the Theotokos our Blessed Virgin Mary as we venerate her across the whole world both East and West.

---

[31] Sergius Bulgakov, *The Burning Bush: On the Orthodox Veneration of the Mother of God* (Grand Rapids, MI: William B. Eerdsman Publishing, 2009), 111.

[32] Anthony Stehlin, *The Prayer Rule of the Theotokos as Prayed by Saint Seraphim of Sarov* (Middletown, DE: Chi Rho Publishing, 2015), iv.

[33] Patricia Ann Kasten, *Lining Your Beads: The Rosaries History, Mysteries, and Prayers* (Huntington, IN: Our Sunday Visitor, 2010), 48.

[34] Ibid., 52-53.

CHAPTER SEVEN

FAITHFULNESS

(*The Word* published "The Holy Diaconate and
The Clarion Call" in January-February 2022.)

After celebrating Mom's 99th birthday in Wauwatosa, Wisconsin, my brother Vince and I boarded a train from Milwaukee and travelled through Chicago to a small town near Fort Wayne, Indiana, our final destination. The train faced some significant stops and dogged delays, and we arrived at the Waterloo train depot two hours late. Despite our fatigue, knowing a hot meal waited for us at home was a source of great consolation. After arriving at my brother's house, I realized it was past midnight, and with our Orthodox Eucharistic fast, I could eat either a warm, wonderful hot dinner right now or Holy Communion later in the morning. The choice was obvious, what my fourth-grade students would call a no-brainer. I went to bed a little hungry, grabbed three hours sleep, and well before dawn drove four hours to All Saints Orthodox Church in Bloomington, Indiana for the Sunday morning Divine Liturgy.

I visit All Saints each summer when I travel up North, as more than a decade ago, it was Father Peter Gillquist of blessed memory who spoke with me after church, at Cracker Barrel with his son Father Peter Jon, and at his home with Khouria Marilyn, these key conversations instrumental to my coming home to Orthodoxy. This summer, after a two-year hiatus because of the pandemic, Father Peter Jon greeted my arrival with an enthusiastic hug. Tired and hungry, I was glad to come to church and looked forward to a simple time of peaceful, behind the scenes worship. Father Peter Jon had other plans, and with his skillful teaching and encouraging guidance, I jumped into the arena when summoned and served my first Divine Liturgy as a Deacon during an Eastern Rite service. The experience was both powerful and heart-altering. I love serving with great joy as a Deacon during Mass at my Western Rite parish in Virginia and now after this wonder-full experience equally treasure in my heart the transcendent beauty of the Eastern Rite Divine Liturgy.

His Eminence Metropolitan Joseph during the Feast of Saint Laurence in 2018 called the diaconate both "historical" and "a holy office" and challenged his Deacons to "listen only to the Word of God in your life and follow it."[35] Our mission and ministry are clear. "The Deacon proclaims the Gospel – he is the leader of the people. The Deacon holds the Chalice at Communion – angels do not touch the Chalice. On behalf of the people, the Deacon touches God."[36]

---

[35] His Eminence Metropolitan Joseph, Western Rite Vicariate Conference, 10 August 2018, St. Peter Orthodox Church, Fort Worth, TX, Lecture.

[36] His Grace Bishop John Abdalah, "Deacons and the Church," Western Rite Vicariate Conference, 9 August 2018, St. Peter Ortho-

With these words, Bishop John encouraged and inspired the Deacons gathered at the 2018 Western Rite Vicariate at Saint Peter Orthodox Church in Fort Worth, Texas.

As an Orthodox Deacon, my most timeless moment during the Divine Liturgy occurs whenever I am called to chant the Holy Gospel. "St. Jerome († 420) speaks of the deacon as reader of the Gospel."[37] Saint Paul advises Saint Timothy, "Preach the word! Be ready in season *and* out of season. Convince, rebuke, exhort, with all longsuffering and teaching."[38] A second source of inestimable joy occurs while holding the Chalice during Holy Communion. Indeed, "there are many witnesses that deacons gave Communion to the faithful, from Justin Martyr through the middle ages down to our own time. We find quite early that the deacon has special charge of the chalice, as St. Lawrence reminded St. Sixtus."[39]

Bishop John spoke to the assembled Deacons about the indescribable wonder of Mystery. At the Transfiguration, the eyes of Peter, James, and John were closed by necessity because they would have been blinded by the glory of Christ. In both "Mystery and Sacrament, God reveals Himself veiled and invisible for His mercy."[40] The Theotokos un-

---

dox Church, Fort Worth, TX, Discussion.

[37] Adrian Fortescue, *The Mass: A Study of the Roman Liturgy*, 2nd ed. (London: Longmans, Green and Co., 1937), 280.

[38] 2 Timothy 4:2 NKJV.

[39] Adrian Fortescue, *The Mass: A Study of the Roman Liturgy*, 374.

[40] His Grace Bishop John Abdalah, "Deacons and the Church," Western Rite Vicariate Conference, 9 August 2018, St. Peter Orthodox Church, Fort Worth, TX, Discussion.

doubtedly understood Mystery and sought the still silence of prayerful contemplation as her constant companion and friend. "Be still and know that I *am* God."[41] Amidst an array of activities during the day, the Blessed Virgin Mary would need to seek God, and He is best found in solitude. God is the ultimate Mystery, and to contemplate this Mystery, Mary sought to be still. As shared by Bishop John, "The Greek noun *mysterion* is linked with the verb *myein*, meaning 'to close the eyes or mouth.' "[42] When we are not talking and stand in silence, we are free to listen. Like the Theotokos, whenever we stand in silence or sit in stillness and close our eyes, we are free to listen to God.

It was both a joy and an honour to be ordained to the Holy Diaconate by Bishop John on the Feast of Saint Patrick at Saint Patrick Orthodox Church in Virginia on Sunday 17 March 2019. The Choir sang: "Ye holy Martyrs, who fought the good fight and hath received thy crowns: entreat ye the Lord, that he will have mercy on our souls. Glory to thee, O Christ our God: the Apostles' boast, the Martyrs' joy, whose preaching was the consubstantial Trinity. O Isaiah, dance thy joy, for a virgin was with child and hath borne a Son, Emmanuel, both God and Man and Orient is His name. Whom magnifying, we call the Virgin blessed."[43] Bishop John added the Prayers of Ordination:

---

[41] Psalm 46:10a NKJV.

[42] Bishop Kallistos Ware, *The Orthodox Way* (Crestwood, NY: St. Vladimir's Seminary Press, 1995), 15.

[43] "The Ordination of a Deacon," *The Ordination of a Deacon | Antiochian Orthodox Christian Archdiocese*, Antiochian Orthodox Christian Archdiocese of North America, ww1.antiochian.

O Lord our God, who by thy foreknowledge dost send down the fullness of the Holy Spirit upon those who are ordained, by Thine inscrutable power, to be thy servitors and to administer thy spotless mysteries: Do thou, the same Master, preserve also this man, whom thou hast been pleased to ordain, through me, by the laying-on of hands, to the service of the Diaconate, in all soberness of life, holding the mystery of the faith in a pure conscience. Vouchsafe unto him the grace which thou didst grant unto Stephen, thy first Martyr, whom, also, thou didst call to be the first in the work of thy ministry; and make him worthy to administer after thy pleasure the degree which it both seemeth good to thee to confer upon him. For they who minister well prepare for themselves a good degree. And manifest him as wholly thy servant. For Thine is the Kingdom and the power and the glory, of the Father and of the Son, and of the Holy Spirit, now and ever, and unto ages of ages, Amen. O God our Savior, who by Thine incorruptible voice didst appoint unto Thine Apostles the law of the Diaconate, and didst manifest the first Martyr, Stephen, to be of the same; and didst proclaim him the first who should exercise the office of a Deacon, as it is written in thy Holy Gospel, "Whosoever desireth to be first among you, let him be your servant": Do thou, O Master of all, fill also this thy servant, who thou hast graciously permitted to enter upon the ministry of a Deacon, with all faith, and love, and power, and holiness, through the inspiration

....
org/1102195079.

of thy Holy and Life-Giving Spirit; for not through the laying-on of my hands, but through the visitation of thy rich bounties, is grace bestowed upon thy worthy ones; that he, being devoid of all sin, may stand blameless before thee in the awesome Day of thy Judgment, and receive the unfailing reward of thy promise. For thou art our God, and unto thee are due all glory, honor, and worship, to the Father and to the Son and to the Holy Spirit, now and ever, and unto ages of ages, Amen.[44]

The Feast of Saint Patrick forever will hold a special place in my heart. As an infant, I was baptized at Saint Patrick Catholic Church in Chesterton, Indiana, very soon after birth. Little did I know I would receive the Holy Chrism as an Orthodox convert fifty-six years later and be ordained as a Deacon sixty-two years later at Saint Patrick Orthodox Church in Bealeton, Virginia.

Whenever I ponder my life today, I recall with fondness a pivotal time in the faith journey leading me home. The most life-changing and lifelong-learning course taken at the University of Notre Dame more than four decades ago was called Theology and Community Service. This seminar, team-taught by Father Don McNeill and Sister Vivian Whitehead, brought about a dozen students into a local nursing home to both learn from and try to minister to the elderly. The main theme of this course is summarized best

---

[44] "The Ordination of a Deacon," *The Ordination of a Deacon | Antiochian Orthodox Christian Archdiocese*, Antiochian Orthodox Christian Archdiocese of North America, ww1.antiochian.org/1102195079.

by this short passage from a now-published draft manuscript serving as our primary textbook for the class: "Compassion asks us to go where it hurts, to enter into places of pain, to share in brokenness, fear, confusion, and anguish. Compassion challenges us to cry out with those in misery, to mourn with those who are lonely, to weep with those in tears. Compassion requires us to be weak with the weak, vulnerable with the vulnerable, and powerless with the powerless. Compassion means full immersion in the condition of being human."[45]

Each student visited two nursing home residents. We would see each of them weekly during the school semester for forty-five minutes. I visited Iris and Joe (not his real name) at a South Bend, Indiana, nursing home. I still recall vividly the strong smell of decay as I walked through the front door to begin my first two visits. I walked into Joe's room first as he sat on the edge of his bed in a dark and gloomy room. I vividly recall his litany of complaints against the nursing home and its staff. Joe hated living at the institution, the staff treated the residents "like dirt," and the food was garbage, the meals so disgusting he would not feed them "to the pigs." Generally optimistic, even overly so, nothing I could say helped break the gloom and doom of our short conversation.

After this somewhat depressing visit, I walked down the hallway and entered Iris' brightly-lit room. A cheerful woman, Iris loved the Lord and enjoyed talking about Jesus. I especially recall a life-size glass dog she enjoyed as if it

---

[45] Henri J. M. Nouwen, Donald P. McNeill, and Douglas A. Morrison, *Compassion* (New York: Doubleday, 1982), 4.

were a real pet. After listening to Joe's harangue, I sheepishly asked Iris about her experiences at the nursing home and expected the worst. Unlike Joe, however, Iris loved living in the nursing home. The nurses and orderlies treated the residents "like kings and queens." Every meal was like "a feast." Iris shared a turning point in her life many years back. When hit with hard times as a young woman, at a point of near despair, doing dishes at the kitchen sink, Iris prayed and received the insight, "There's always darkness before the dawn." She laughed at and overcame her sadness at the time and instead felt immense joy. Since that religious experience many years earlier, Iris' life was transformed towards the good, and her life and outlook were never the same.

I began writing extensively in a journal throughout my semester-long nursing home visits and continued this practice for many years, completing close to two dozen lengthy journals during a little more than a decade. The focus of this course was compassion. Answering one of my journal entries, Sister Vivian describes compassion with concrete clarity: "God is compassion – We try to be compassionate realizing that the actual power of our compassion is because our God is compassionate. Jesus came to tell us by who He was and the way He lived that our God is compassionate. We come in the 20th century to say by who we are and the way we live that our God is compassionate."[46]

This God of empathy calls each of us to a special vocation. "Likewise deacons *must be* reverent, not dou-

---

[46] Sister Vivian Whitehead, 12 October 1978, Theology and Community Service, University of Notre Dame, Notre Dame, IN, Journal Comment.

ble-tongued, not given to much wine, not greedy for money, holding the mystery of the faith with a pure conscience."[47] At the Western Rite Vicariate Conference, Bishop John asked us to name some of the most notable Deacons in Church History: Saint Laurence recognized the poor as "the treasures of the Church" and suggested his captors "turn me over, I am done"; Saint Athanasius "was a deacon at the First Ecumenical Council"; Saint Ephrem "wrote hymns" and "did not want to become a priest"; and Saint Stephen was "the first martyr."[48] The Holy Diaconate began when the Twelve Apostles selected Stephen and six companions after declaring, "Wherefore, brethren, look ye out among you seven men of honest report, full of the Holy Ghost and wisdom, whom we may appoint over this business."[49] The first Deacons ministered to the neglected Greek widows and served tables.[50]

At his ordination, called to embrace fully the ministry of service and the virtue of compassion, the Deacon receives the Stole, the Dalmatic, and the Gospel Book.[51] At Saint Patrick Orthodox Church, the clergy say special prayers while dressing with each of the Sacred Vestments in preparing to serve at the Holy Altar during Mass. The holy Stole worn

---

[47] 1 Timothy 3:8-9 NKJV.

[48] His Grace Bishop John Abdalah, "Deacons and the Church," Western Rite Vicariate Conference, 9 August 2018, St. Peter Orthodox Church, Fort Worth, TX, Discussion.

[49] Acts 6:3 KJV.

[50] Acts 6:1-2 KJV.

[51] His Grace Bishop John Abdalah, "Deacons and the Church," Western Rite Vicariate Conference, 9 August 2018, St. Peter Orthodox Church, Fort Worth, TX, Discussion.

by Priests and Deacons is kissed and then placed around the neck with this solemn prayer, "Give me again, O Lord, the stole of immortality, which I lost by the transgression of my first parents, and although I am unworthy to come unto Thy Holy Sacrament, grant that I may attain everlasting felicity."[52] Truly none of us is worthy to stand on such holy ground by the Holy Altar surrounded by the saints and the heavenly hosts.

The icon of Saint John the Baptist graces every Orthodox Church. Until the public ministry of Jesus, Saint John was the most popular preacher of his day. Some wondered if he was the Messiah. "John answered them, saying, I baptize with water: but there standeth one among you, whom ye know not; He it is, who coming after me is preferred before me, whose shoe's latchet I am not worthy to unloose."[53] Surely in the mud and grime of the walkways by the Jordan River, travelled by man and beast alike, one's sandals or shoes would be filthy. Within the households of the day, perhaps one of the lowest chores for a servant would be removing and cleaning the master's filthy footwear. Compared to Christ, Saint John the Baptist became the lowest of the slaves. "He must increase, but I *must* decrease."[54] The Deacon is called to embrace this holy humility.

---

[52] "The Prayers to be Said While Vesting," Saint Patrick Orthodox Church Sacristy, from Dom Gaspar Lefebvre, *The Saint Andrew Daily Missal* (Great Falls, MT: St. Bonaventure Publications, 1999), 946.

[53] John 1:26-27 KJV.

[54] John 3:30 KJV.

The Ordination of the Deacon concludes with these bold and powerful proclamations from the Bishop and the congregation:

Bishop: HE IS WORTHY!
People: HE IS WORTHY!
Bishop: MUSTAHEK!
People: MUSTAHEK!
Bishop: AXIOS!
People: AXIOS!
People: AXIOS![55]

These declarations deeply touch yet also trouble my heart. A few of us are called into the clergy, yet only God is worthy. Only through His infinite grace and abundant blessing could we possibly be called worthy. Within our Western Rite Divine Liturgy, before receiving the Body and Blood of Christ in the Eucharist, we confess our utter unworthiness to accept such a miraculous, wonder-full gift with the words similarly spoken to Jesus by a faithful Roman soldier in Capernaum: "The centurion answered and said, Lord, I am not worthy that thou shouldest come under my roof: but speak the word only, and my servant shall be healed."[56] I am not worthy, but with God's Word, I accept the call to the holy diaconate with joyful humility.

I have felt a deep and abiding call to the priesthood since fourth grade:

---

[55] "The Ordination of a Deacon," *The Ordination of a Deacon | Antiochian Orthodox Christian Archdiocese*, Antiochian Orthodox Christian Archdiocese of North America, ww1.antiochian.org/1102195079.

[56] Matthew 8:8 KJV.

> My frame was not hidden from You,
> When I was made in secret,
> *And* skillfully wrought in the depths of the earth;
> Your eyes have seen my unformed substance;
> And in Your book were all written
> The days that were ordained *for me*,
> When as yet there was not one of them.[57]

As I reflect on my past pastoral ministry experiences and discern God's call in my life, these words of His Eminence Metropolitan Philip of thrice-blessed memory are most inspiring: "Priesthood is not a job; it is a *vocation*. Priesthood is not a profession; it is a covenant between the priest and his parish."[58] Just as the incarnate Christ was fully God and fully man, both God and bondservant, so too are we called to bring the light of Jesus our God into the hearts of hurting people, uniting the divine with the human. The priest's mission is to lead His people to Jesus Christ. As Metropolitan Philip directed his priests, "You were ordained in order to bring Christ to people and people to Christ."[59]

With much joy, I came home into the Orthodox Church late in life. Passing sixty years of age, I may no longer be eligible for priestly ordination, and this emptiness becomes God's will for my life. Yet the dream still lives in my heart. Although my calling may not be humanly possible, "with

---

[57] Psalm 139:15-16 KJV.
[58] Joseph J. Allen, ed., *And He Leads Them* (Ben Lomond, CA: Conciliar Press, 2001), 244 (emphasis in original).
[59] Joseph J. Allen, ed., *Orthodox Synthesis: The Unity of Theological Thought* (Crestwood, NY: St. Vladimir's Seminary Press, 1981), 95.

God nothing shall be impossible."[60] So I continue to "watch and pray"[61] with hope, trusting the continued power and presence of God's will for my life. "For surely I know the plans I have for you, says the LORD, plans for your welfare and not for harm, to give you a future with hope."[62]

If God wants me to become an Orthodox priest, He will open the door. In the meantime, trusting God fully and seeking His will, serving as an Orthodox Deacon during the Divine Liturgy at the best church in the world brings an abundance of joy to my heart. His Eminence Metropolitan Joseph during the Feast of Saint Laurence challenged his Deacons to "listen only to the Word of God in your life and follow it."[63] Filled with Jesus as the Truth and the truth of the Word of God, we quiet our still hearts and strive to worship our Triune God with awe and wonder. "For that stillness of the soul from the world naturally arouses a slight stirring of thoughts in the soul, that by them it may be lifted to God and remain in wonder."[64] This diaconate declaration from Metropolitan Joseph applies to all Orthodox Christians: "Read Scripture as if it flows from your whole heart, your whole being. Let it sanctify you and other people."[65] Those of

---

[60] Luke 1:37 KJV.

[61] Matthew 26:41 KJV.

[62] Jeremiah 29:11 NRSV.

[63] His Eminence Metropolitan Joseph, Western Rite Vicariate Conference, 10 August 2018, St. Peter Orthodox Church, Fort Worth, TX, Lecture.

[64] Saint Isaac of Nineveh, *On Ascetic Life*, translated by Mary Hansbury (Crestwood, NY: St. Vladimir's Seminary Press, 1989), 43.

[65] His Eminence Metropolitan Joseph, Western Rite Vicariate Conference, 10 August 2018, St. Peter Orthodox Church, Fort Worth,

us called into the Holy Diaconate enthusiastically embrace this clarion call.

BIBLIOGRAPHY

Abdalah, His Grace Bishop John. "Deacons and the Church." Western Rite Vicariate Conference. 9 August 2018. St. Peter Orthodox Church, Fort Worth, TX. Discussion.

Allen, Joseph J. ed. *And He Leads Them*. Ben Lomond, CA: Conciliar Press, 2001.

_____. *Orthodox Synthesis: The Unity of Theological Thought*. Crestwood, NY: St. Vladimir's Seminary Press, 1981.

Fortescue, Adrian. *The Mass: A Study of the Roman Liturgy*, 2nd ed. London: Longmans, Green and Co., 1937.

Isaac of Nineveh, Saint. *On Ascetic Life*, translated by Mary Hansbury. Crestwood, NY: St. Vladimir's Seminary Press, 1989.

Joseph, His Eminence Metropolitan. Western Rite Vicariate Conference. 10 August 2018. St. Peter Orthodox Church, Fort Worth, TX. Lecture.

Lochbihler, David. (1978). Theology and Community Service. University of Notre Dame, Notre Dame, IN. Journal Entry.

Nouwen, Henri J. M., Donald P. McNeill, and Douglas A. Morrison. *Compassion*. New York: Doubleday, 1982.

The New Testament in Four Versions: King James, Revised Standard, Phillips Modern English, New English Bible. Washington, DC: Christianity Today, 1963.

"The Ordination of a Deacon." *The Ordination of a Deacon | Antiochian Orthodox Christian Archdiocese*. Antiochian Orthodox Christian Archdiocese of North America. ww1.antiochian.org/1102195079.

The Orthodox Study Bible. Nashville, TN: Thomas Nelson Publishers, 2008.

The Orthodox Study Bible: New Testament and Psalms. Nashville, TN: Thomas Nelson Publishers, 1993.

Ware, Bishop Kallistos. *The Orthodox Way*. Crestwood, NY: St. Vladimir's Seminary Press, 1995.

Whitehead, Sister Vivian. (1978). Theology and Community Service. University of Notre Dame, Notre Dame, IN. Journal Comment.

CHAPTER EIGHT

GENTLENESS

A global pandemic rocked our world.

I was blessed. Mom after getting vaccinated began playing cards with her friends in Wauwatosa, Wisconsin, again. My church with courage and grace worshipped together, added converts, and nurtured friendships. My school, mandated by the State to do daily temperature checks, wear masks, and social distance, captured a Virginia state basketball championship. We did not miss a single day in the classroom, and despite rigid government restrictions, not one of my fantastic fourth graders whined or complained.

Yet not everyone was so blessed. One lifelong friend from New York, a city stunned by the ferocity of this dreaded disease in the very early days of the pandemic, lost dozens of family members and close friends. Some of our friends lost someone. Still other friends contracted the disease, suffered, and recovered. Too many of our friends lost their jobs and their livelihoods, facing financial ruin. Nations around the world, from Great Britain to Germany, from Italy to India, from Egypt to Ethiopia, from Brazil to Bangladesh, were brought to their knees by tragic tears and our great mutual enemy, death.

After the nationwide spring shutdown, with our academic fourth quarter online, I was blessed beyond measure beginning the following August to worship freely and not miss a single day of teaching in the classroom throughout the pandemic. Others were not so lucky, battling this disease, losing their jobs, or attending school online. Many of us spent more time at home than usual, masked at the local grocery store and faced with the ultimate decision in battling adversity in life: Given these circumstances, do I choose to become bitter or better?

Which leads to the choice ultimately facing all of us, either during a global pandemic or upon facing disease and our inevitable deathbed: Do I choose joy or bitterness? We all are dying, and death is the ultimate solitude. Call it what you will, but upon facing death, even if we are surrounded by loving family and lifelong friends, we die alone.

Or do we?

Prior to our Pentecost Vigil morning service, with the baptismal font and Mass preparations readied, I sat in the Sacristy at Saint Patrick Orthodox Church in Virginia with Subdeacon John Wiley and acolyte Kai. We discussed the essence and depth of silence and solitude.

"Now in the morning, having risen a long while before daylight, He went out and departed to a solitary place; and there He prayed."[66] Jesus grew up with a wonderful family and was intimately immersed in His faith. Despite being engaged in a busy and active ministry, Jesus experienced a profound and ongoing union and communion with His

---

[66] Mark 1:35 NKJV.

Heavenly Father. Why do our busy lives make it so difficult to fulfil this inner yearning for prayer? During our Sacristy conversation, Subdeacon John Wiley eloquently said, "Our whole lives today are structured to distract us from personal reflection."[67] From our ever-ringing iPhones, the interesting things on our iPads, and the wide reach of social media, television, and movies, it is not surprising we are distracted, and it is difficult to pray. Jesus prayed in still silence and encountered God. In our hectic and hurried lives, is it any surprise that we cannot?

Perhaps you strive to seek God with a quiet walk in the woods. The poet Gerard Manley Hopkins beheld the beauty of nature and declared, "The world is charged with the grandeur of God."[68] Even when we walk in wonder, however, our minds beholding God's grandeur still face the incessant interruption of our typical tyrannical thoughts. This walk in the woods though special is not still silence.

Perhaps you will decide to read a superb Orthodox theological book written by one of the giants of our faith like Father Joseph Allen, Father Peter Gillquist, Father Vladimir Lossky, and Father Alexander Schmemann, four superb Orthodox authors, all of blessed memory, penning multiple manuscripts well-read by so many of us and sitting in our bookshelves.

Subdeacon John Wiley made an excellent point during our Sacristy pre-liturgical discussion: Even while doing such

---

[67] Subdeacon John Wiley Gebhardt, Saint Patrick Orthodox Church, Bealeton, Virginia, 19 June 2021.

[68] Gerard Manley Hopkins, *Poems of Gerard Manley Hopkins*, ed. W. H. Gardner (New York: Oxford University Press, 1948), 70.

a great thing like reading some of our finest Orthodox authors, with our minds actively engaged, this is not still silence. Our minds although enriched are far from silent; they are active and engaged. Reading is good yet not still silence.

There must be another way to encounter God. Surely all of us worshiping within the Orthodox Church, the truest and dearest community of faith, can discover the silence and stillness of deep and abiding prayer in our lives.

Perhaps you pray *Lectio Divina* in the Monastic Diurnal. You speak slowly, you try to concentrate. Yet your mind still may wander. Your Diurnal ribbons may be misplaced and needing to be moved. You read the Psalms yet if asked immediately afterwards, you have no recollection of what you have just read. Father Edward Hughes challenged us during a Lenten Retreat several years ago to pray our next Divine Office as if it were our last. I fail to do this. God loves our effort, we try to do our best, yet this is not still silence.

Perhaps you will sit in your favourite chair at home or on the porch and just try to pray to God with no distractions. There is no noise, there seems to be silence. Yet often when I do this, my mind is still racing, filled with an overabundance of random thoughts. I do try to pray, yet is my prayer directed to God, or am I only talking to myself? This attempt at prayer though valiant is not still silence.

Perhaps this is what we seek, this is what we want deep down inside: "Be still, and know that I am God."[69] We need to slow down. We need to stop. We need to rest. We need to empty our minds moving a million miles a minute. To be-

---

[69] Psalm 46:10a KJV.

gin our earnest and eternal quest towards God, our Triune Trinity shrouded in indescribable mystery – Our Heavenly Father omnipresent yet hidden, our Crucified and Risen Christ fully divine and fully human, our Holy Ghost the Pure Paraclete – we need to first simply seek to be still. After stillness follows silence:

> My soul, wait in silence for God only,
> For my hope is from Him.[70]

For me, the key word within this verse is "wait." Not just try to be silent, but to "wait in silence." For truly, "my hope is from Him," and prayer is not about us, but all about Him. Waiting in silence, striving for stillness, is a good first step. "But you, when you pray, go into your room, and when you have shut your door, pray to your Father who *is* in the secret *place*; and your Father who sees in secret will reward you openly."[71]

Author Kyriacos Markides in *The Mountain of Silence* follows Father Maximos, a Mount Athos monk, around Cyprus. He learned there is a great difference between loneliness and being alone. Father Maximos expressed this difference in describing a meeting with a man living in almost completely isolation. "I remember years ago I met a hermit on Mount Athos who lived by himself in the wilderness. I asked him, 'Father, aren't you afraid to live here all alone?' His reply was that he could never feel alone since he con-

---

[70] Psalm 62:5 NASB.
[71] Matthew 6:6 NKJV.

tinuously prayed. He was filled with the living presence of God's love."[72]

Subdeacon John Wiley expressed it best. "The key to finding joyful solitude is silence before God."[73] We experience in still silence deep joy, fervent prayer, and Eucharistic thanksgiving. "Rejoice evermore. Pray without ceasing. In every thing give thanks: for this is the will of God in Christ Jesus concerning you."[74] To begin to try to discover still silence, I only can offer two humble suggestions.

First, when you receive the Eucharist, strive to embrace the miracle of the moment and still your heart. Second, as you go to sleep at night, with your head on the pillow after another grueling day at work while facing ongoing challenges raising your children in Christ at home, perhaps with the Jesus Prayer or a prayer to Our Lady, strive to both quiet your busy mind and seek still silence until you fall asleep. "Now it came to pass in those days that He went out to the mountain to pray, and continued all night in prayer to God."[75]

In still silence, we stop talking and start listening. When our minds race, we try to remember the Body and Blood of Christ. When distractions assail us, we try instead to focus on the Name of Jesus or the Love of Our Lady. God is infinite, we are finite, and we can never fully arrive. Yet by trying our best each day, with sincere hearts, our ever-present

---

[72] Kyriacos C. Markides, *The Mountain of Silence* (New York: Doubleday, 2001), 202-203.

[73] Subdeacon John Wiley Gebhardt, 19 June 2021.

[74] 1 Thessalonians 5:16-18 KJV.

[75] Luke 6:12 NKJV.

Father is there and meets us right wherever and whenever we seek to stand in still silence:

> And he said, Go forth, and stand upon the mount before the LORD. And, behold, the LORD passed by, and a great and strong wind rent the mountains, and brake in pieces the rocks before the LORD; *but* the LORD *was* not in the earthquake: And after the earthquake a fire; *but* the LORD *was* not in the fire: and after the fire a still small voice.[76]

Becoming Orthodox opens one's world to wonder like never before. "And now here is my secret, a very simple secret: It is only with the heart that one can see rightly; what is essential is invisible to the eye."[77] With these words, Antoine de Saint-Exupéry describes the essence of seeing our world through the inner eyes of faith. This ongoing quest for the essential and the invisible aptly expresses our lifelong journey towards still silence. God is always there, patiently waiting. Baptized in the Blessed Water, anointed with the Chrism Oil, receiving the Body and Blood of Christ during the Divine Liturgy, we may be facing suffering, pain, and death, yet because of our Orthodox faith, God is with us, and we are never alone.

"Truly I say to you, unless you are converted and become like children, you shall not enter the kingdom of heaven."[78]

---

[76] 1 Kings 19:11-12 KJV.
[77] Antoine de Saint-Exupéry, *The Little Prince* (San Diego: Harcourt Brace, 1971), 73.
[78] Matthew 18:3 NASB.

To be a child of God means to see again with the inner eyes of faith, to truly wonder. A child is devoted to his or her best friends Jesus and Mary with a pure heart and the experience of joyful humility. Wrapping up our Sacristy sacred session, I asked twelve-year-old acolyte Kai what he thought, and he responded with superb simplicity, "I like this conversation."[79]

BIBLIOGRAPHY

Friedrich, Kai. Saint Patrick Orthodox Church. Bealeton, Virginia. 19 June 2021.

Gebhardt, Subdeacon John Wiley. Saint Patrick Orthodox Church. Bealeton, Virginia. 19 June 2021.

Hopkins, Gerard Manley. *Poems of Gerard Manley Hopkins*, 3rd ed., edited by W. H. Gardner. New York & London: Oxford University Press, 1948.

Markides, Kyriacos C. *The Mountain of Silence.* New York: Doubleday, 2001.

Saint-Exupéry, Antoine de. *The Little Prince.* San Diego: Harcourt Brace, 1971.

---

[79] Kai Friedrich, Saint Patrick Orthodox Church, Bealeton, Virginia, 19 June 2021.

CHAPTER NINE

SELF-CONTROL

Doubly blessed to serve as a Deacon both at Saint Patrick Orthodox Church in Virginia, a Western Rite parish in the Eastern Orthodox Church, and at the Holy Altar with Father Peter Jon Gillquist at All Saints Orthodox Church in Indiana for the first time at an Eastern Rite Divine Liturgy during a recent family vacation. The Divine Liturgies both East and West are timeless experiences of "heaven on earth."[80]

As a Wesleyan pastor in southern Indiana prior to coming home to Orthodoxy more than a decade ago, I celebrated our simple Christmas Eve service at our little church in 2009 and was blessed beyond measure. On other occasions, I spent hours with Bobby, a World War Two veteran and former P.O.W. captured by Nazi Germany, sharing the Good News of Jesus Christ during visits at his home. I hoped these talks would build a personal relationship with him, with the goal of eventually bringing him back into our church. Only a few attended our Christmas Eve service that night, but amazingly, Bobby was one of them, and that brought great

---

[80] Alexander Schmemann, *For the Life of the World*, 2nd ed. rev. (Crestwood, NY: St. Vladimir's Seminary Press, 1973), 30.

joy to my heart. This was the only time I ever saw him in church, and a few months later I preached his funeral.

That Christmas Eve was meaningful for another reason. I yearned for many days and even during our evening service to go to Midnight Mass that night. I decided to continue this long-treasured tradition, begun in my Roman Catholic childhood, with a late-night journey to Saint Michael Orthodox Church in Louisville, Kentucky, for their Christmas Eve service once the last of my congregation left our church earlier that evening.

The Nativity Eve Divine Liturgy at Saint Michael Orthodox Church in Louisville brought me back to both the gold and glitter and the magnificence and mystery of my childhood faith. The very next day, I drove back to Louisville to attend Lauds at the Saint George Chapel and found myself surprised we were all standing with no chairs, and I was lost completely during the service. Father Alexander Atty of blessed memory came to my assistance and generously offered his copy of the Daily Service book for me to keep.

Father Alexander showed kindness to me that morning and in several other encounters during the next few years as he battled the scourge of cancer with courage and grace. I once asked him specifically what he wanted me to pray for during his illness, and he thought for a few seconds before responding, "Peace. Praying for healing gets old after a while."[81] On another occasion Father Thomas Palke of Saint Raphael of Brooklyn Orthodox Church invited me to hear Father Alexander address his congregation, and he spoke

---

[81] Alexander Atty, "The Prodigal Son," Vespers, Saint Raphael of Brooklyn Orthodox Church, Chantilly, VA, 24 March 2012. Lecture.

eloquently about the Prodigal Son. Father Alexander talked about how earlier he was going to face a ten-hour cancer surgery with the thought that he "may not make it." He engaged in a most powerful life confession lasting three to four hours and concluded his talk to us by saying, "Illness was a great gift to me. God gave me a great gift: cancer. It taught me to prepare for death every day."[82]

My Indiana Wesleyan pastorate brought an additional encounter with Orthodoxy. I was honoured and humbled to meet Father Peter Gillquist of blessed memory at All Saints Orthodox Church in nearby Bloomington, Indiana. At the Cracker Barrel in Bloomington, with Father Peter and his son Father Peter Jon, he spoke lovingly about the Blessed Virgin Mary, rekindling another deep love from my childhood long-dormant during my Protestant pastoral assignments. Father Peter saw the Theotokos in the Burning Bush and in other Scriptural passages in the Old Testament, another startling viewpoint I never previously considered.

At the end of our meal, I shared with Father Peter and Father Peter Jon about the next phase of my spiritual journey as I would be returning soon to serve as an assistant pastor at a Wesleyan Church in Virginia. Father Peter wrote down for me the names of two Antiochian priests, Father Patrick Cardine of Saint Patrick Orthodox Church and Father Thomas Palke of Saint Raphael of Brooklyn Orthodox Church. Visiting both churches, I loved celebrating both the Eastern Rite Divine Liturgy at Saint Raphael and the Western Rite Mass at Saint Patrick, and both men played

---

[82] Ibid.

a pivotal role by inspiring me to pursue Orthodoxy. I continued to "watch and pray"[83] with hope, trusting the power and presence of God's will for my life. "For surely I know the plans I have for you, says the Lord, plans for your welfare and not for harm, to give you a future with hope."[84] Securing a teaching and coaching assignment in Northern Virginia, I moved to Warrenton, Virginia, a small town where Saint Patrick as a mission church worshipped walking distance away in a rented space in the back of a large antique store. Although loving the Divine Liturgies in both the East and West, God guided me to live next to and learn best the Western Rite Liturgy.

The Holy Orthodox Church throughout the world is united in theology yet also richly blessed by the emergence of diverse, historic liturgical expressions. The Eastern Rite Divine Liturgy and the Western Rite Mass are each beautiful and timeless in their own unique ways. "The two names that are most commonly used among Orthodox Western Rite congregations to describe the Eucharistic gathering are the Mass, and the Divine Liturgy."[85] More than a decade has passed since my move from Indiana to Virginia, and on Saturday 31 July 2021, Saint Patrick Orthodox Church hosted the Western Rite Vicariate Conference entitled "Conversations on Atonement." This essay will present a theological discussion of atonement from our Western Rite conference.

---

[83] Matthew 26:41 KJV.

[84] Jeremiah 29:11 NRSV.

[85] Michael D. Keiser, *Offering the Lamb: Reflections on the Western Rite Mass in the Orthodox Church* (Bloomington, IN: AuthorHouse, 2006), 9-10.

We began with Gregorian Chant Lauds followed by our Western Rite Solemn High Mass with His Grace Bishop John Abdalah. Our two featured speakers were Father Patrick Henry Reardon and Doctor Marcus Plested, to be followed by a Question-Answer Session featuring Bishop John, Doctor Plested, Father Edward Hughes, Father John Fenton, and Father Patrick Cardine. The conference concluded with Vespers and Benediction, and we celebrated the Western Rite Lauds and Mass on Sunday.

Our opening Saturday Lauds was dedicated to Our Lady the Theotokos: "He created me from the beginning before the world, and I shall never fail. In the holy tabernacle I served before him (Ecclesiasticus 24:9-10). Bishop John soon preached the sermon during Mass. Even if you "look deep down in your heart for human love, it will not be enough." Although the world tells us we "deserve happiness and pleasure," real happiness consists in "knowing the tomb of Christ is empty." Bishop John once encountered "a cat who thought she was a dog. The cat would bark at me!" This barking cat clearly was out of sorts and in turmoil. This troubled cat seemed unhappy as a cat and instead acted like a dog. Bishop John summarized this part of his sermon, "Cats are only going to be happy if they know they are cats. Humans are going to be happy by acting in the image and likeness of God because that's who we are meant to be."[86]

Father Patrick Henry Reardon shared his reflections about atonement during our first session while being in-

---

[86] His Grace Bishop John Abdalah, Western Rite Vicariate Conference, 31 July 2021, St. Patrick Orthodox Church, Bealeton, VA, Sermon.

terviewed by Father John Fenton and Father Patrick Cardine. He focused upon the prayers of Jesus to His Heavenly Father, like this example: "At that time Jesus answered and said, I thank thee, O Father, Lord of heaven and earth, because thou hast hid these things from the wise and prudent, and hast revealed them unto babes. Even so, Father; for it seemed good in thy sight."[87] Jesus told the people, "All things are delivered unto me of my Father: and no man knoweth the Son, but the Father; neither knoweth any man the Father, save the Son, and *he* to whomsoever the Son will reveal *him*."[88] The premier prayer from Jesus to God the Father occurs in John 17, referred to by biblical scholars as "Jesus' High-Priestly Prayer."[89] As stated by Father Reardon, "Only Christ is related to God as Father." Beginning with Jesus' relationship with God, only Jesus understands fully what the words in His prayers to the Father actually mean. "The only one who knows God is Jesus." Recognizing our prayer often centers on ourselves, Father Patrick Henry Reardon challenged us to contemplate the mysterious by seeking to go into the "self-consciousness of Jesus."[90]

The two interviewers provided additional insight and depth. After receiving an answer describing how special Psalms help inform this inside view of the mind of Christ,

---

[87] Matthew 11:25-26 KJV.

[88] Matthew 11:27 KJV.

[89] Paul Nadim Tarazi, *The New Testament: An Introduction, vol. 3, Johannine Writings* (Crestwood, NY: St. Vladimir's Seminary Press, 2004), 230.

[90] Father Patrick Henry Reardon, Western Rite Vicariate Conference, 31 July 2021, St. Patrick Orthodox Church, Bealeton, VA, Session One Interview.

Father John Fenton added how Psalms 3 (4), 21 (22), 30 (31), 68 (69), and 73 (74) suggested by Father Reardon "help us get into the inside of Christ."[91] Father Patrick Cardine offered a final thought. As we consider "Jesus' inner life with the Father, we pray to get into the mind of Christ. What is Jesus thinking as we get into the mind of Christ as He prays to the Father on the inside?"[92] As finite beings we cannot even begin to understand the infinite mind of Christ. Yet as this first session was summarized by Father Reardon, "Jesus' self-concept is the door to the Father."[93]

Father Patrick Henry Reardon helped us understand atonement as our union and communion with God. The second session, a lecture by Doctor Marcus Plested, built upon this theme of being one with God by focusing on the theological concepts of theosis and deification. "Grace and power be multiplied to you in the knowledge of God and of Jesus our Lord, as His divine power has given to us all things that *pertain* to life and godliness, through the knowledge of Him who called us by glory and virtue, by which have been given to us exceedingly great and precious promises, that through these you may be partakers of the divine nature,

---

[91] Father John Fenton, Western Rite Vicariate Conference, 31 July 2021, St. Patrick Orthodox Church, Bealeton, VA, Session One Interview.

[92] Father Patrick Cardine, Western Rite Vicariate Conference, 31 July 2021, St. Patrick Orthodox Church, Bealeton, VA, Session One Interview.

[93] Father Patrick Henry Reardon, Western Rite Vicariate Conference, 31 July 2021, St. Patrick Orthodox Church, Bealeton, VA, Session One Interview.

having escaped the corruption *that is* in the world through lust."[94]

Doctor Plested described the etymology of atonement as being "English in origin," as there is "no equivalent" to this theological term "in any other language." Atonement is "AT-ONE-MENT" and involves "bringing together" or to "bring into union." Christ prayed so that all could be one: "Neither pray I for these alone, but for them also which shall believe on me through their word; That they all may be one; as thou, Father *art* in me, and I in thee, that they also may be one in us: that the world may believe that thou hast sent me."[95] Doctor Plested described theosis as at-one-ment.

Whereas Saint Nicholas Cabasilas considered the "sacraments as a way to theosis," Saint Gregory Palamas perceived the "Jesus Prayer as a way to theosis." Saint Nicholas Cabasilas describes the Eucharistic path to theosis or our at-one-ment as union with God: "Since Jesus, being of twofold nature, in accordance with His humanity which He shares with us honoured the Father and wove for Him that wondrous crown of glory from His Body and Blood, Christ's Body then is the only medicine against sin and His Blood the only ransom from offenses."[96] Similarly, as stated by Doctor Plested, Saint Gregory Palamas distinguished between "God as He is (essence) and God as He reveals Himself (attributes, activities, energies)." Whereas Palamas

---

[94] 2 Peter 1:2-4 NKJV.

[95] John 17:20-21 KJV.

[96] Nicholas Cabasilas, *The Life in Christ*, translated by Carmino J. deCatanzaro (Crestwood, NY: St. Vladimir's Seminary Press, 1974), 120.

responded "ad hoc to attacks" against the Jesus Prayer or Prayer of the Heart, "Cabasilas complements Palamas by putting atonement in a sacramental context." Doctor Plested concluded by linking "theosis as atonement."[97]

The Western Rite Vicariate Conference continued with a Question & Answer session, with each panelist adding some interesting insights. We learned there are many ways to understand atonement. Bishop John reminded us the consequences of sin is death, and for this reason Christ died on the Cross. "God has given the Church as a way of participating in his love and life."[98] Father Edward Hughes took this a step further, challenging us to "conform our prayer life to the liturgical life of the Church."[99] Father John Fenton added, Jesus became "human for the sake of atonement."[100] Father Patrick Cardine shared how "God's wrath is against sin, not against us. We are expiated or purged of sin. Yet God's feelings of wrath against sin remains."[101] The positive rather than punitive element of atonement was shared admirably by Doctor Michael Plested, as there is "no better

---

[97] Doctor Marcus Plested, Western Rite Vicariate Conference, 31 July 2021, St. Patrick Orthodox Church, Bealeton, VA, Session Two Lecture.

[98] Bishop John Abdalah, Western Rite Vicariate Conference, 31 July 2021, St. Patrick Orthodox Church, Bealeton, VA, Session Three Q & A.

[99] Father Edward Hughes, Western Rite Vicariate Conference, 31 July 2021, St. Patrick Orthodox Church, Bealeton, VA, Session Three Q & A.

[100] Father John Fenton, Western Rite Vicariate Conference, 31 July 2021, St. Patrick Orthodox Church, Bealeton, VA, Session Three Q & A.

[101] Father Patrick Cardine, Western Rite Vicariate Conference, 31 July 2021, St. Patrick Orthodox Church, Bealeton, VA, Session Three Q & A.

way of showing love" than by giving your "life for the beloved, uniting with the beloved."[102]

Bishop John spoke to our Saint Patrick community and guests during the Sunday morning Divine Liturgy, known in the Western Rite Orthodox tradition as the Mass. Atonement offers the opportunity of "being more connected and at-one-ness with Him." Because "salvation means sharing God's life, we need to be willing to get past our intellect and our pleasures, to get past ourselves to unite ourselves to Him who is true." Besides being "very grateful to everyone who made this weekend possible," Bishop John concluded his sermon with these most gracious words: "This has been a phenomenal weekend. I thank God for this."[103]

BIBLIOGRAPHY

Abdalah, His Grace Bishop John. Western Rite Vicariate Conference. 31 July 2021. St. Patrick Orthodox Church, Bealeton, VA. Sermon.

Cabasilas, Nicholas. *The Life in Christ*, translated by Carmino J. deCatanzaro. Crestwood, NY: St. Vladimir's Seminary Press, 1974).

---

[102] Dr. Michael Plested, Western Rite Vicariate Conference, 31 July 2021, St. Patrick Orthodox Church, Bealeton, VA, Session Three Q & A.

[103] Bishop John Abdalah, Western Rite Vicariate Conference, 1 August 2021, St. Patrick Orthodox Church, Bealeton, VA, Sermon.

Cardine, Father Patrick. Western Rite Vicariate Conference. 31 July 2021. St. Patrick Orthodox Church, Bealeton, VA. Session One Interview.

Keiser, Michael D. *Offering the Lamb: Reflections on the Western Rite Mass in the Orthodox Church.* Bloomington, IN: AuthorHouse, 2006.

The New Testament in Four Versions: King James, Revised Standard, Phillips Modern English, New English Bible. Washington, DC: Christianity Today, 1963.

The Orthodox Study Bible. Nashville, TN: Thomas Nelson Publishers, 1982.

Plested, Doctor Marcus. Western Rite Vicariate Conference. 31 July 2021. St. Patrick Orthodox Church, Bealeton, VA. Session Two Lecture.

Reardon, Father Patrick Henry. Western Rite Vicariate Conference. 31 July 2021, St. Patrick Orthodox Church, Bealeton, VA, Session One Interview.

Schmemann, Alexander. *For the Life of the World*, 2nd ed. rev. Crestwood, NY: St. Vladimir's Seminary Press, 1973.

Tarazi, Paul Nadim. *The New Testament: An Introduction. Vol. 3, Johannine Writings.* Crestwood, NY: St. Vladimir's Seminary Press, 2004.

COMMENCEMENT IN CHRIST

(The Author delivered this Commencement Address
at The Fairfax Christian School in May 2022.)

I recently delivered the High School Commencement Address at The Fairfax Christian School in Dulles, Virginia, where I am blessed to teach fourth grade. Here is my speech to the Class of 2022 graduating seniors.

Presbyterian clergyman Robert L. Thoburn with God's grace launched our school on the ground floor of a large Victorian home, kindergarten through eighth grade, in September of 1961. John F. Kennedy was President, the Beatles were only one-year old, and very few Americans could find Vietnam on a globe.

A half-century later, the Senate of Virginia in an official Joint Resolution celebrated the life and legacy of the Honorable Robert Loren Thoburn, a minister, an educator, and a former member of the Virginia House of Delegates upon his falling asleep on the twenty-third of December in 2012. Besides helping to found the first Orthodox Presbyterian Church in Northern Virginia, "Bob Thoburn founded Fairfax Christian School to provide a rigorous academic curriculum… in a wholesome Christian environment." The Virginia Senate called Bob "a devoted family man… fondly remembered by his wife, Rosemary," his eight children, his forty-six grandchildren, and his nineteen great-grandchildren. A blessed family rich in faith leaving a legacy of love.

We as educators follow our founder's advice and "strive to teach effectively." Education "is the responsibility of the home. We ought, therefore, to work closely with parents, to be grateful for any extra work they do at home with their children, and we should realize that they are really the boss."

Parents, we truly love you and thank you for giving us this privilege to teach your wonderful children, our brilliant graduates. And graduates, make sure you thank your parents and grandparents for their love and sacrifice in teaching you and sending you to your superb school.

This being my first Commencement Address, I read an old speech I once heard many years ago and asked my family and friends what they would share with the Class of 2022. My oldest brother Fred delivered the Valedictorian Speech at the University of Notre Dame in 1973. That speech and that on-campus visit inspired me to follow in his footprints, go to Notre Dame, and become a Chicago attorney. Fred's words from nearly fifty years ago were quite remarkable. He called his classmates "brothers and sisters under the divine gaze." His closing remarks to the Notre Dame Class of 1973 apply equally as well to the Fairfax Christian Class of 2022. He told his classmates:

"As our Lord instructed, we must become leaven of society, the vital catalyst which can affect the genuine liberation of an entire nation in a respect for truth and in an ultimate concern for love. My friends, our path stands clear.

"We who have been liberated must accept the urgent challenge of our living faith and make the lives of our brothers and sisters our own. The sacrifices may be many, but the rewards will be great, both in this world and the one which is to come."

My sister Lyn the doctor always did exceptionally well in school. She encourages all of you "to make straight A's in this: Going to heaven." She added, "Nothing else in life matters." My brother Vince offered this advice, "The rich man is not the one who has the most but the one who needs the least."

A dear friend of mine from Indiana, Khouria Marilyn Gillquist, wrote this to me, "Jesus Christ is the same yesterday, today, and forever. Hebrews 13:8." She added, "I remember in my college experience being so confused by the many philosophies presented to me. It seemed everything was changing, and that is surely the case today. What an assurance to know that God does not change… and He is our Rock."

I also did some research about the long, rich history of our illustrious school. The *Washington Post* featured this headline in 1981:

NO-FRILLS ACADEMY THRIVES IN FAIRFAX

Deacon Douglas from my church offered this advice to you: "Run your life the way your school has been run: minimize self-indulgent frills; maximize respect for others; zero in on clear objectives; and demand accountability of yourself."

Sixth-grader Catarina wanted you to hear Psalm 105:1. "Give thanks to the LORD, call upon His name; Make His deeds known among the peoples." Her advice: "You are going off to college. Spread the Word of God when you go."

Fourth-grader Jacquelyn wanted you to hear Proverbs 3:5-6:

> Trust in the LORD with all your heart
> And do not lean on your own understanding.
> In all your ways acknowledge Him,
> And He will make your paths straight.

Finally, I called my mom to get her advice. Mom turns one hundred in August. She told me on Sunday, "This is what your Dad would say: Do nothing to harm anyone, and you will have no regrets."

Following all their leads, here is my advice to you, the Fairfax Christian School Class of 2022: Love and live the Bible as you love Jesus and live for Him.

Like Jesus, live a life of humility. Philippians 2:3.

> Let nothing be done through selfish ambition or conceit, but in lowliness of mind let each esteem others better than himself. Though He was in the form of God, Jesus did not deem equality with God something to be grasped; rather, He emptied Himself and took the form of a slave, being born in the likeness of man. He was known to be of human estate, and it was thus that He humbled Himself, obediently accepting death, death on a Cross.

Be like Jesus: Live a life of humility. Also like Jesus, live a life of service. Matthew 25.

When the Son of Man comes in His glory, and all the holy angels with Him, then He will sit on the throne of His glory. Then the King will say to those on His right hand, "Come, you blessed of My Father, inherit the kingdom prepared for you from the foundation of the world.

> For I was hungry, and you gave me food;
> I was thirsty, and you gave me drink;
> I was a stranger, and you invited me in;
> I was naked, and you clothed me;
> I was sick, and you visited me;
> I was in prison, and you came to me."

From World Vision: Globally, about 8.9% of the world's population – 690 million people – go to bed on an empty stomach each night. By the time some of you graduate from law school in 2030 – 840 million people in our world will go to bed hungry every night.

After my first year at the University of Texas School of Law, I served as a law clerk at the Navajo Nation in Chinle, Arizona. The poverty I witnessed was unbelievable. A lot of homes or hogans did not even have running water. I visited the Navajoland Nursing Home on weekends, the only nursing home in the entire Navajo Nation. Two distinct memories from forty years ago come readily to mind.

I visited a young man a little older than you in the nursing home. How did a 22-year-old land in a home for the elderly and infirm? He drank too much – he drove his car – he got in an accident – he lost the use of his legs. He made some really bad choices and ended up in a nursing home.

I also visited a very old Navajo man at the same nursing home. He seemed like a distinguished and honorable man. He probably worked very hard his entire life. As I entered his room, I quickly noticed something very unusual. He literally was washing his hands in the clear water of the toilet. Many Navajo homes did not even have running water. This may have been the first time this man had seen things like a sink or a toilet. Simple things we take for granted. Simple things many in our world simply do not have. Like fresh water and enough food.

Be like Jesus: Live a life of service. Feed the hungry. Give water to the thirsty. Visit prisoners and care for the sick in hospitals and nursing homes.

Like Jesus – live humbly – serve others – and live a life of purity. Matthew 5:8. "Blessed are the pure in heart, for they shall see God." Psalm 51:10. "Create in me a pure heart, O God. And renew a right spirit within me." Psalm 119:9. "How shall a young person stay on the path of purity? By living according to your word."

"By living according to your word."

If I could give one bit of advice to the Class of 2022, it would be this: Like Jesus, live and love God's Word – Sacred Scripture – the Holy Bible – make it a part of your daily life. Read a chapter every day. Commit to memory verses that touch your heart. Find an app to read the Bible in a year, about twenty minutes a day. Finally, find one life verse that summarizes and epitomizes who you are in Christ.

Some of you have been at our school since kindergarten. A great life verse might be your school's motto. Proverbs

9:10. "Wisdom begins with respect for the Lord." My favourite verse, the words of Jesus. John 6:56. "He who eats my flesh and drinks my blood abides in me, and I in him." A close second, the words of John the Baptist, talking about Jesus. John 3:30. "He must increase, but I must decrease."

Here are some other great verses. Matthew 28:19. "Therefore, go and make disciples of all nations, baptizing them in the name of the Father and of the Son and of the Holy Spirit." Imagine the astonishing impact of your life if you make this your lifelong goal or mission.

Maybe your vision of your future is not so clear. A great life verse for you might be Jeremiah 29:11. "For I know the plans that I have for you," declares the LORD, "plans for prosperity and not for disaster, to give you a future and a hope."

Imagine going into every academic test or every basketball or volleyball game with this as your life verse. Philippians 4:13. "I can do all things through Christ who strengthens me."

And consider this: Your life will be enhanced and enriched to the degree you bring the Holy Trinity into your heart. God the Father – "You shall love the Lord your God with all your heart, with all your soul, and with all your mind." God the Son – "He is despised and rejected of men; a man of sorrows and acquainted with grief: and we hid as it were our faces from him; he was despised, and we esteemed him not." God the Holy Spirit – Here is my favourite prayer to the Holy Spirit: "O Holy Spirit, beloved of my soul, I adore you. Enlighten me, guide me, strengthen me, console me. Tell me what I should do, give me your orders.

I promise to submit myself to all that you desire of me and to accept all that you let happen to me. Let me only know your will" (Cardinal Désiré-Joseph Mercier).

One of my most memorable classes at the University of Notre Dame was called Theology and Community Service. Meeting as a seminar, each student also once a week visited two elderly nursing home residents. I vividly recall the exact moment I first entered the nursing home in South Bend, Indiana. I walked inside the double doors more than forty years ago, and I still can see myself, a little older than you, walking into the building to be both stunned and shocked by the smell – such a vivid memory – the smell of sickness, death, and decay.

I visited Victor and Iris for the very first time during my senior year at Notre Dame, a great senior year because Joe Montana was our quarterback. Victor was sitting on the side of his bed. The curtains were drawn, and the room was somewhat dark and gloomy as we struck up a conversation. I asked him a few questions like, "How do you like living here?"

Victor said, "I hate it here."

I asked, "How are the people working here?"

Victor said, "Horrible. They're very mean. They treat us like dirt."

I tried to find something to cheer him up a little, to find some silver lining. I asked him, "How is the food?"

I remember Victor's answer from more than forty years ago like it was yesterday. "The food is terrible here. I wouldn't feed this slop to pigs."

We spoke for about forty minutes, and to this day I still recall Victor's answers to those three questions. As I left his room, I was as depressed as Victor! These nursing home visits were going to be a lot tougher than I thought.

Then I walked down a couple hallways into Iris' much brighter room. It was a beautiful day outside, and you could see the light through the window. I asked Iris the same three questions posed to Victor. After my first depressing visit, I was expecting the worst. Yet Iris' smile was as bright as her small, sunny room.

I asked Iris, "How do you like it here?"

Iris smiled as she said, "I love it here."

I asked her, "How about the nurses and aides? Are they friendly?"

Iris said, "They treat us like kings and queens."

I asked Iris if she likes the nursing home food. She practically beamed as she said, "Every meal is like a feast."

Two people. Their rooms fifty yards apart. One room bright and sunny, the other room dark and gloomy. Two older folks with two totally different attitudes.

Iris told me once that many years ago, she and her husband, not too much older than you, were in dire financial straits. Nothing was going right in their young lives, and they were really struggling. She was doing the dishes one day, at the sink, looking outside the kitchen window, in despair. And somehow, from somewhere, this thought popped into her mind and heart: "There's always darkness before the dawn." A smile crossed her face, and Iris began singing. Jesus was the source of her joy. And Iris never looked back.

We kept in touch for ten years after that very special senior year at Notre Dame. I was working at a downtown

Chicago law firm when I got the phone call from her family letting me know that Iris had fallen asleep in the Lord.

Every year I ask my fourth graders, as I now ask you to think and consider: At what age in her long life did Iris nurture and learn to be joyful and optimistic? And at what age in life did Victor move towards his negative attitude of pessimism and despair? Most fourth graders guess their attitudes were formed when they were older, in their forties or their sixties. Although we do not know for sure, my best guess is that their attitudes were formed during their middle or high school years. Maybe when they were a little younger than you.

I can just see Victor in middle school many years ago.

"How do you like your school?"

"I hate it here."

"What about your teachers?"

"They are so mean to us."

"How is the food in the cafeteria?"

"Terrible."

And I can see Iris graduating from high school, perhaps from the Class of 1922. "I just love my school. The teachers are so nice. And the cafeteria food is the best." Attitude is everything. Attitudes formed right now as seniors in high school will last a lifetime.

Fairfax Christian School Class of 2022. My message to you: Decide and declare and demonstrate the attitude you want to nurture for the rest of your life – right now – this very summer – choose to walk the narrow and right path in life – the way of Jesus – the way of goodness and light, the way of love and joy.

And reject, utterly reject, the way of the world, the wide road of doubt and despair – pride and pessimism – cynicism and sin. Live humbly. Serve others. Stay pure. Strive to be holy in Christ. Love God with your whole heart, mind, soul, and strength. Love your neighbor as yourself. Pray for the grace to even love your enemies. Love and forgive one another.

From my brother Vince, Ephesians 4:32. "Be kind to one another, compassionate, forgiving each other, just as God in Christ also has forgiven you."

Dedicate your life to God's Holy Word. Read the Bible. Study the Bible. Memorize the Bible. Pray the Bible. Love the Bible.

Fairfax Christian School Class of 2022: Say yes to Jesus like never before. Live and love in His strength – with His abundant power – and with His infinite and Amazing Grace.

EPILOGUE

THE JOY OF ORTHODOXY

Again, the kingdom of heaven is like treasure hidden in
a field, which a man found and hid; and for joy over it he
goes and sells all that he has and buys that field
(Matthew 13:44 NKJV).

Mom, living a full century and recently celebrating her one hundredth birthday with family and friends this past summer, called me at school one autumn day while I was teaching my fourth-grade scholars. We are not supposed to take personal calls at school, but even in the middle of a lesson, when you see there is a telephone call from your one-hundred-year-old mother, you pick up.

Mom wanted me to know she just had read my first devotional book *Prayers to Our Lady East and West* for the third time. With Mom on the telephone in front of seventeen enthusiastic fourth-graders for the first time ever during my three-decade teaching career, a great idea popped into my head. "Hey, everybody, let's all sing *Happy Birthday* to my mom. She just turned one hundred this summer!"

My fourth graders sang loudly and magnificently.

Like priests preparing a sermon, authors often pray and ponder in order to discover their next topic. Later that day, back with my fourth graders right after lunch in the early afternoon, Langley, whose parents purchased my first book about Our Lady, asked whether I would write another book. Thinking out loud, I said something like, "I am looking for a new book idea. For months I have been trying to think of one but have not been able to come up with anything." Langley thought of a great idea and wrote it down. She shared how Jesus died on the Cross and rose from the dead, walking to a weeping Mary Magdalene by the tomb. Langley suggested a "maybe title" for a future book, *The Joyfulness of Jesus*. This article begins this journey of joy.

As a fourth-grade teacher, my mind drifted back to my own fourth-grade year at Saint Charles Catholic School in Fort Wayne, Indiana. Around that time of my early childhood, I recall reading a short story about baseball during class one day. The batter hit a sharp ground ball directly towards an infielder. Alert and ready to field the grounder, the shortstop crouched and waited for the hard-hit ball to reach his glove. All of a sudden, the baseball hit a tiny rock on the infield ground, took a funny, high hop, and hit the shortstop right in his face. The runner reached first base on the shortstop's error.

Rubbing his injured forehead, the shortstop was furious. He grabbed the pebble causing the bad bounce and got ready to heave it off the diamond towards the dugout. Instead, he noticed the pebble was shiny. He slipped it into his pocket.

After the game, heading home, the ballplayer looked more closely at the shiny pebble. Low and behold, the pebble was actually a gold nugget. The very next day, the player withdrew every single dollar he had saved in the bank and purchased the baseball field. The man discovered gold on his land.

I discovered pure gold a decade ago upon discovering Orthodoxy. My life has never been the same.

For the first five decades of my life, despite growing up Roman Catholic and earning an advanced theological degree, it did not register within my consciousness that an Orthodox Church even existed. The timeless truths of the Orthodox Church completely escaped my narrow worldview.

Coaching and teaching in Northern Virginia two decades ago, my Christian school closed her doors after many decades as a successful church-school ministry. I interviewed for a new classroom assignment at a school called Little Flock associated with Saint Mark Coptic Orthodox Church in Fairfax. This job interview with Father Anthony Messeh completely changed the direction of my life. He sketched a timeline dating from the time of Christ to the 21st century. The line began as one, yet after a millennium, the line split with one wing branching to the right. This line turning to the side was the Roman Catholic Church, and after another half-millennium, this veering branch sprouted hundreds of smaller branches. These multiple branches portrayed the Protestant Reformation. Yet the single straight line from the Apostles walking with Jesus in the first century continued unimpeded to the top of the page. This single, straight line represented the Orthodox Church.

I recall my immediate reaction. Just prior to this teaching interview, I just had been ordained to preach the Gospel!

More than sixteen years later, I remember exactly what I said to this Coptic priest. "Father Anthony, if what you say is true, my entire worldview is destroyed."

Father Anthony generously gave five Orthodox books to me. After a couple years, I became lead pastor at a fine Wesleyan church in Southern Indiana. I loved preaching about the Word of God, leading the youth group, and visiting some older folks in their homes for lengthy conversations. I would drive for nearly an hour to a Roman Catholic seminary library to spend twenty hours a week researching and preparing my weekly sermons. Delving into Sacred Scripture so deeply brought great joy to my heart. Yet a sense of being incomplete, an emptiness inside, remained. After five years of sitting silently on one of my bookshelves, these five books were remembered. I began reading. One of the five Orthodox books from Father Anthony spoke a simple message: "Come and see."

Saint Augustine in his *Confessions* stated, "You have made us for yourself, O Lord, and our hearts are restless until they rest in you." During our Christmas Eve Wesleyan church service years ago, our small gathering of thirteen folks was blessed beyond measure as an elderly gentleman graced our pews for the first time in many, many years. Yet my heart was restless. Thinking back half-a-century to my Roman Catholic childhood, I missed the joyful simplicity and beauty of Midnight Mass. After wishing a Merry Christmas to my flock, I drove across state lines to Louisville, Kentucky, to attend the Nativity Eve Divine Liturgy at Saint Michael Orthodox Church. The joyful mystery of my early childhood faith returned.

"Come and see." During subsequent visits to Orthodox churches in the area, I was blessed to meet and converse with two holy heroes of blessed memory, Father Alexander Atty at Saint Michael and Father Peter Gillquist at All Saints Orthodox Church in Bloomington, Indiana. The Divine Liturgies were so beautiful. One All Saints parishioner shared how timeless these services seemed to her as we walked at nearby McCormick's Creek State Park. Father Alexander was especially kind as I stumbled my way through Lauds. Father Peter and his son Father Peter Jon met with me at Cracker Barrel, and each summer I would meet Father Peter and subsequently his wife Khouria Marilyn to talk more about our respective family and faith journeys.

The joy of faith and family truly inspires. My Dad of blessed memory and I used to play these baseball card and strategy games all the time when I was a kid. I remember he used to crush me in the regular season, but during the World Series, I somehow managed to win. Looking back years later, I really am convinced in my heart Dad let me win.

I held Dad's hand when he fell asleep. Nearly forty years have passed, and I still think of him most every day. His World War Two scrapbook is a staple in my fourth-grade classroom. Mom at one hundred is still going strong and winning at cards, and I am finalizing the paperwork to secure Dad's old Army discharge papers so that when the inevitable happens, Mom and Dad shall sit side-by-side at Arlington National Cemetery.

My weekly talks with Mom focus a lot upon our family days together, me being the youngest of four kids born and raised two years apart at 3525 Elwood Drive in Fort Wayne, Indiana, during the tumultuous 1960s. I still remember our old telephone number, Trinity 3-9373, and our walking two blocks to attend Saint Charles Borromeo Catholic Church and School during my eight grade school years.

Speaking with Mom this past Christmas, we talked about a wonder-filled visit she recently shared with Father Ciprian Sas and his wife Presvytera Maggie from the Orthodox Church situated right next door to Mom's independent living complex. Annunciation Greek Orthodox Church in Wauwatosa, Wisconsin, was built by the famous architect Frank Lloyd Wright. Right after getting married after World War Two, Mom and Dad lived in a Frank Lloyd Wright house just off Lake Michigan.

Way back during my childhood, Dad and I would arrive at Midnight Mass (the cool guitar Mass at the Crosier seminary) ninety minutes early to get the good seats. When I was a pastor in Southern Indiana, a yearning for Midnight Mass began my journey into Orthodoxy. This past Christmas, our Saint Patrick Midnight Mass was at 10:00pm, and I arrived home around 1:30am after the sacristy talks and set my alarm so I could begin opening the many gifts from my family, friends, and fourth graders at 4:00am like we did at 3525 Elwood Drive on Christmas morning more than half-a-century ago.

"The Divine Liturgy is an indescribably magnificent feast."[104] Within our Orthodox tradition, "Feast means *joy*."[105]

---

[104] David Lochbihler, *The Joy of Orthodoxy* (Netherlands: Orthodox Logos, 2022), 20.

[105] Alexander Schmemann, *For the Life of the World* (Crestwood,

Our Midnight Mass at Saint Patrick this year was timeless and beautiful as are all our Divine Liturgies throughout the entire Orthodox world.

> To see a World in a grain of sand,
> And a Heaven in a wild flower,
> Hold Infinity in the palm of your hand,
> And Eternity in an hour.[106]

At Saint Patrick in Virginia's calm countryside... at Annunciation in Wisconsin... at All Saints in Indiana... at Saint Michael in Kentucky... at Saint Mark Coptic by the busy D.C. Beltway in Virginia... during each Divine Liturgy, heaven meets earth in our Orthodox churches around the world, and our hearts experience eternity during a seemingly timeless several hours. "I have seen the God-given task with which the sons of men are to be occupied. He has made everything beautiful in its time. Also He has put eternity in their hearts, except that no one can find out the work that God does from beginning to end" (Ecclesiastes 3:10-11 NKJV). Our Orthodox Divine Liturgy is both transcendent and eternal. With immeasurable joy, we truly hold eternity in an hour.

NY: St. Vladimir's Seminary Press, 1973), 63 (emphasis in original).

[106] William Blake, "Auguries of Innocence," *The Poetical Works of William Blake*, ed. John Sampson (London: Oxford University, 1934), 171.

ABOUT THE AUTHOR

Deacon David Lochbihler, J.D., serves at the Holy Altar at Saint Patrick Orthodox Church and teaches Fourth Grade at The Fairfax Christian School in Virginia. After graduating *summa cum laude* from the University of Notre Dame and *cum laude* from the University of Texas School of Law, Deacon David worked as a Chicago attorney for three years before becoming a teacher and coach for three decades. He also earned three Master's degrees in Elementary Education, Biblical Studies, and Orthodox Theology. His varsity high school basketball and soccer teams captured four N.V.I.A.C. conference championships. He authored *Prayers to Our Lady East and West* (2021), *The Joy of Orthodoxy* (2022), *Our Orthodox Holy Family: A Joyful Journey with Jesus and Mary* (2022), and *Joyful Solitude* (2023).

DEACON DAVID LOCHBIHLER, J.D.

OUR ORTHODOX HOLY FAMILY:
A JOYFUL JOURNEY WITH JESUS AND MARY

ORTHODOX LOGOS PUBLISHING

PRAYERS
TO OUR LADY
EAST AND WEST

DEACON DAVID LOCHBIHLER, J.D.

ORTHODOX LOGOS PUBLISHING

DEACON DAVID LOCHBIHLER, J.D.

JOYFUL SOLITUDE

ORTHODOX LOGOS PUBLISHING

Uitgeverij Orthodox Logos

- *De Orthodoxe Kerk: Verleden en heden* – Jean Meyendorff
- *Biecht en communie* – Alexander Schmemann
- *Verliefd Zijn op het Leven* – Samensteller: Maxim Hodak
- *De Orthodoxe Kerk* – Aartspriester Sergei Hackel
- *De mensenrechten in het licht van het Evangelie* – Nicolas Lossky
- *Geboren in Haat Herboren in Liefde* – Klaus Kenneth
- *Hegoumena Thaissia van Leouchino: brieven aan een novice*
- *Het Jezusgebed* – Een monnik van de oosterse kerk
- *Gebedenboek Voor Kinderen: Volgens De Orthodox Christelijke Traditie*
- *Dagboek Van Keizerin Alexandra* – Keizerin Alexandra
- *Mijn ontmoeting met Archimandriet Sophrony* – Aartspriester Silouan Osseel
- *Stap voor stap veranderen* – Vader Meletios Webber
- *De Weg Naar Binnen* – Metropoliet Anthony (Bloom) Van Sourozh
- *Geraakt door God's liefde* – Klooster van de Levenschenkende Bron Chania
- *De Heilige Silouan de Athoniet* – Archimandrite Sophrony
- *The Beatitudes: A Pathway to Theosis* – Christopher J. Mertens
- *De Kracht van de Naam* – Metropoliet Kallistos van Diokleia
- *De Orthodoxe Weg* – Metropoliet Kallistos van Diokleia
- *Serafim Van Sarov* – Irina Goraïnoff
- *Feesten van de Orthodoxe Kerk - een Leerzaam Kleurboek*
- *Catechetisch woord Over Het gebed van het Hart* – Aartspreiester Silouan Osseel
- *Naar de Eenheid?* – Leonide Ouspensky
- *Bidden Met Ikonen* – Jim Forest

- *Onze Gedachten Bepalen Ons Leven* – Vader Thaddeus Van Vitovnica
- *Alledaagse Heiligen En Andere Verhalen* – Archimandriet Tichon (Sjevkoenov)
- *Geestelijke Brieven* – Vader Jozef De Hesychast
- *Nihilisme* – Vader Serafim Rose
- *Gods Openbaring Aan Het Menselijk Hart* – Vader Serafim Rose
- *In De Kaukazus* – Monnik Merkurius
- *Terugkeer* – Archimandriet Nektarios Antonopoulos
- *Weest ook gij uitgebreid* – Archimandriet Zacharias (Zacharou)
- *De Orthodoxe Kerk* – Verleden en heden

- *Fruit of the Spirit: An Orthodox Anthology* – Deacon David Lochbihler, J.D.
- *Joyful Solitude* – Deacon David Lochbihler, J.D.
- *Our Orthodox Holy Family* – Deacon David Lochbihler, J.D.
- *Prayers to Our Lady East and West* – Deacon David Lochbihler, J.D.
- *The Joy of Orthodoxy* – Deacon David Lochbihler, J.D.
- *The Inner Cohesion between the Bible and the Fathers in Byzantine Tradition* – S.M. Roye
- *St. Germanus of Auxerre* – Howard Huws
- *Elder Anthimos Of Saint Anne's* – Dr. Charalambos M. Bousias
- *Orthodox Preaching as the Oral Icon of Christ* – James Kenneth Hamrick
- *The Final Kingdom* – Pyotr Volkov

www.orthodoxlogos.com

www.ingramcontent.com/pod-product-compliance
Lightning Source LLC
Chambersburg PA
CBHW031122080526
44587CB00011B/1075